WORLD CREATURES

A COLORING BOOK FOR KIDS

BY @bestprodesigner

THIS COLORING BOOK

BELONGS TO :

LADYBUG

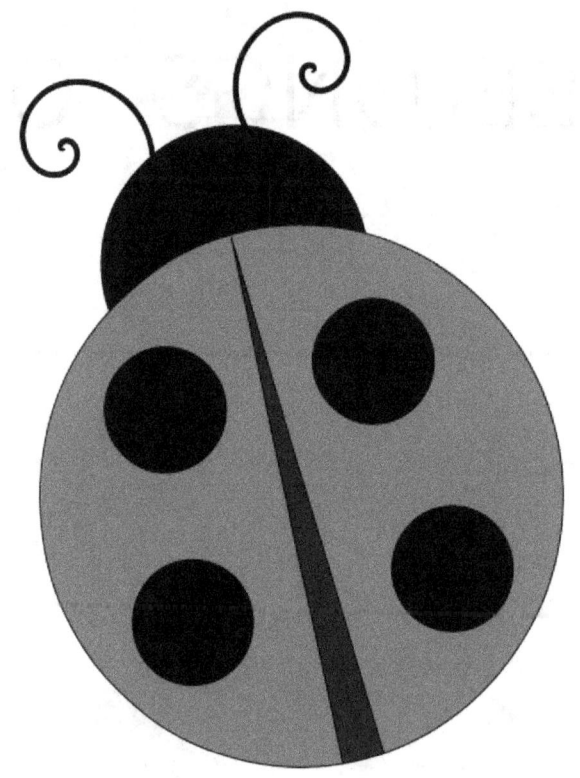

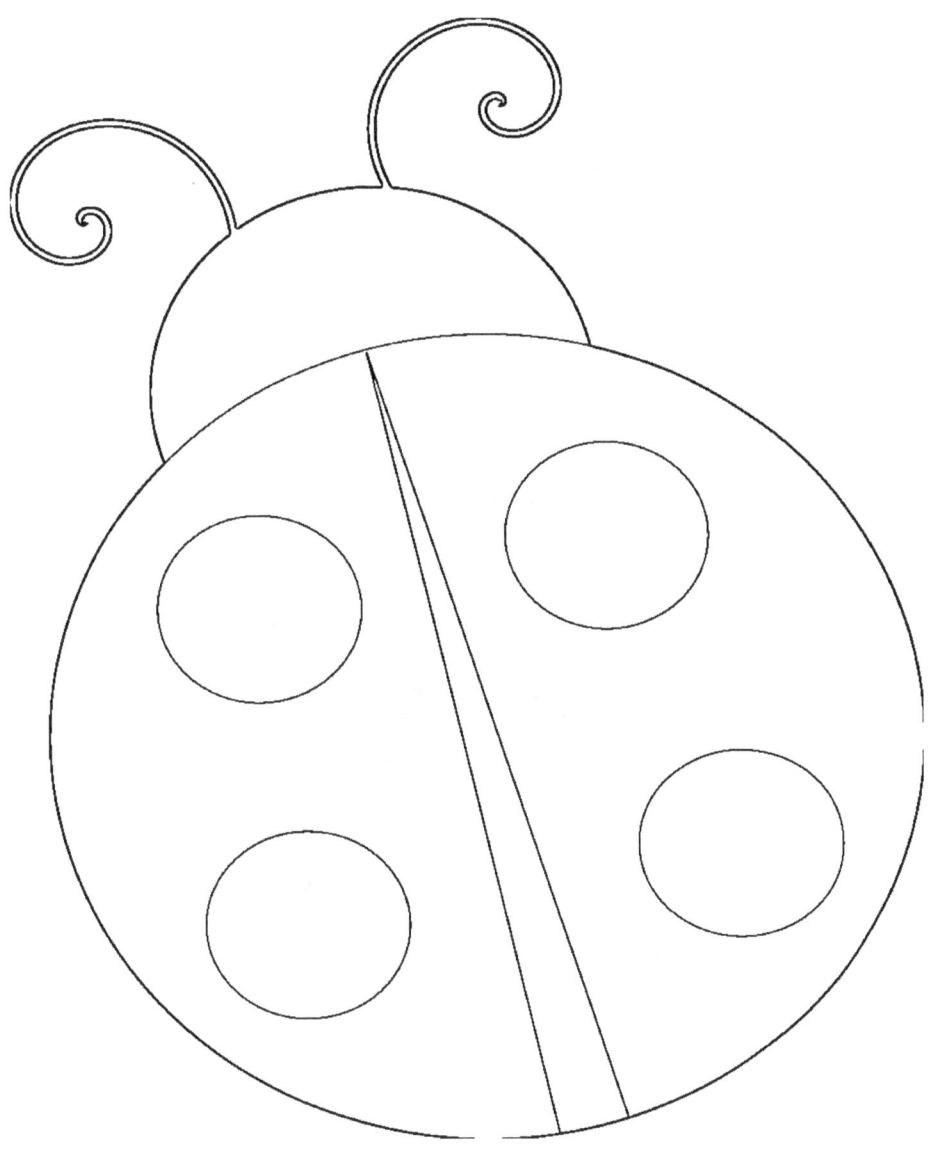

CHICK

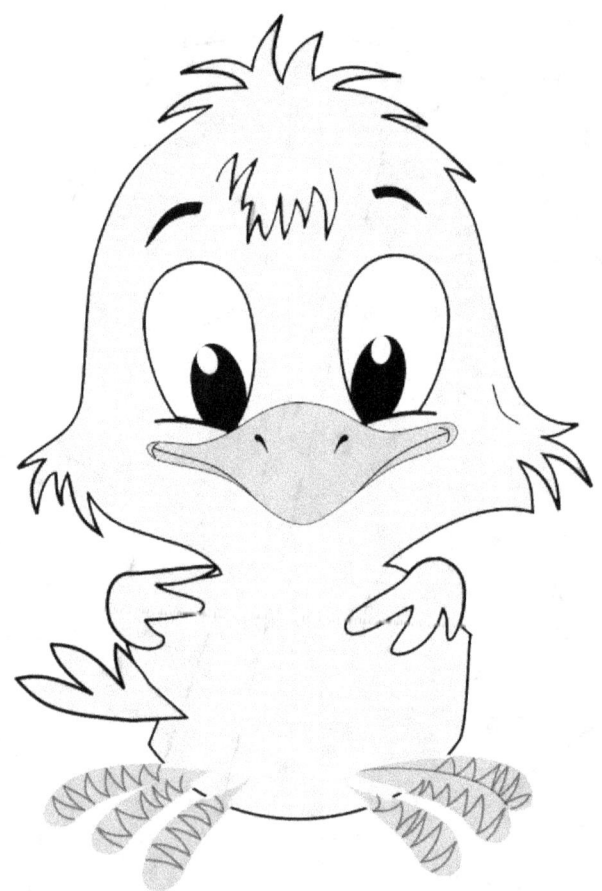

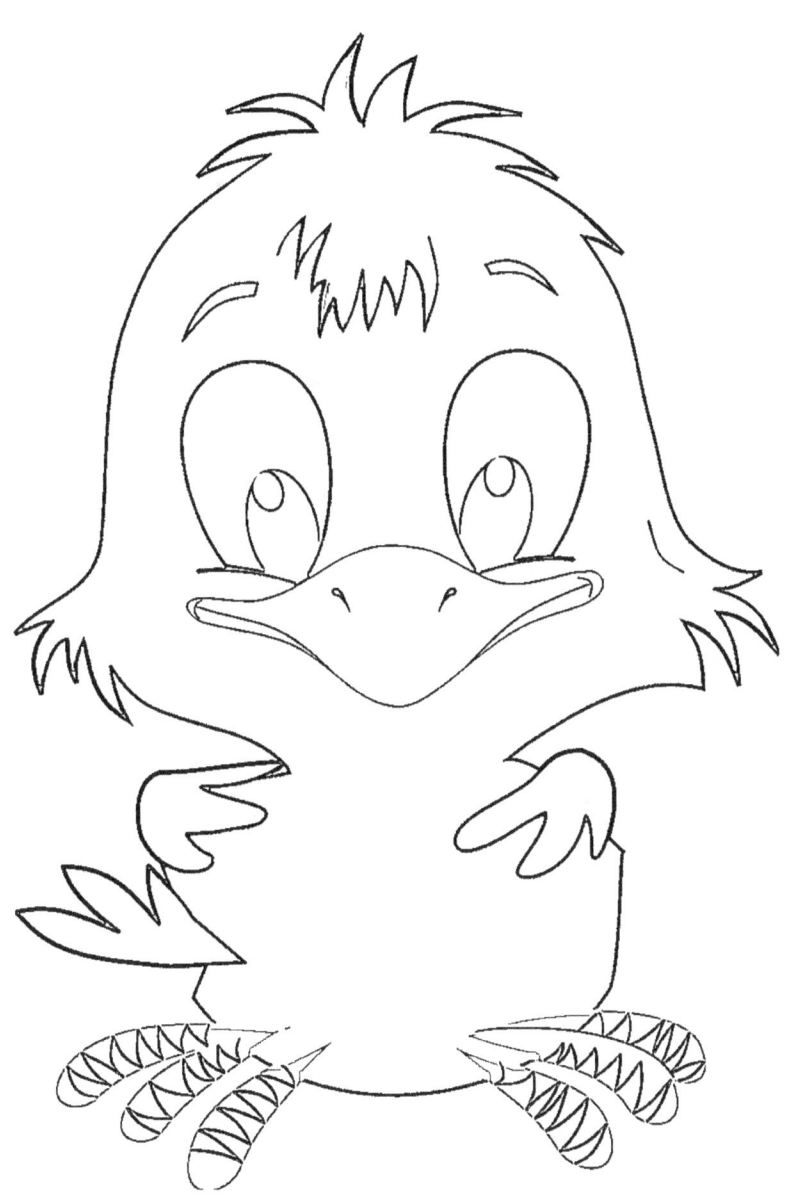

BEE

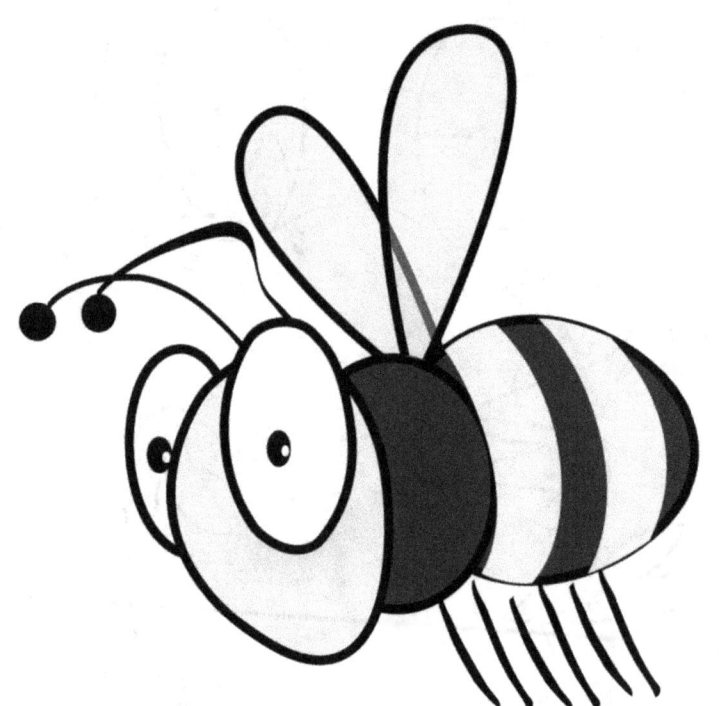

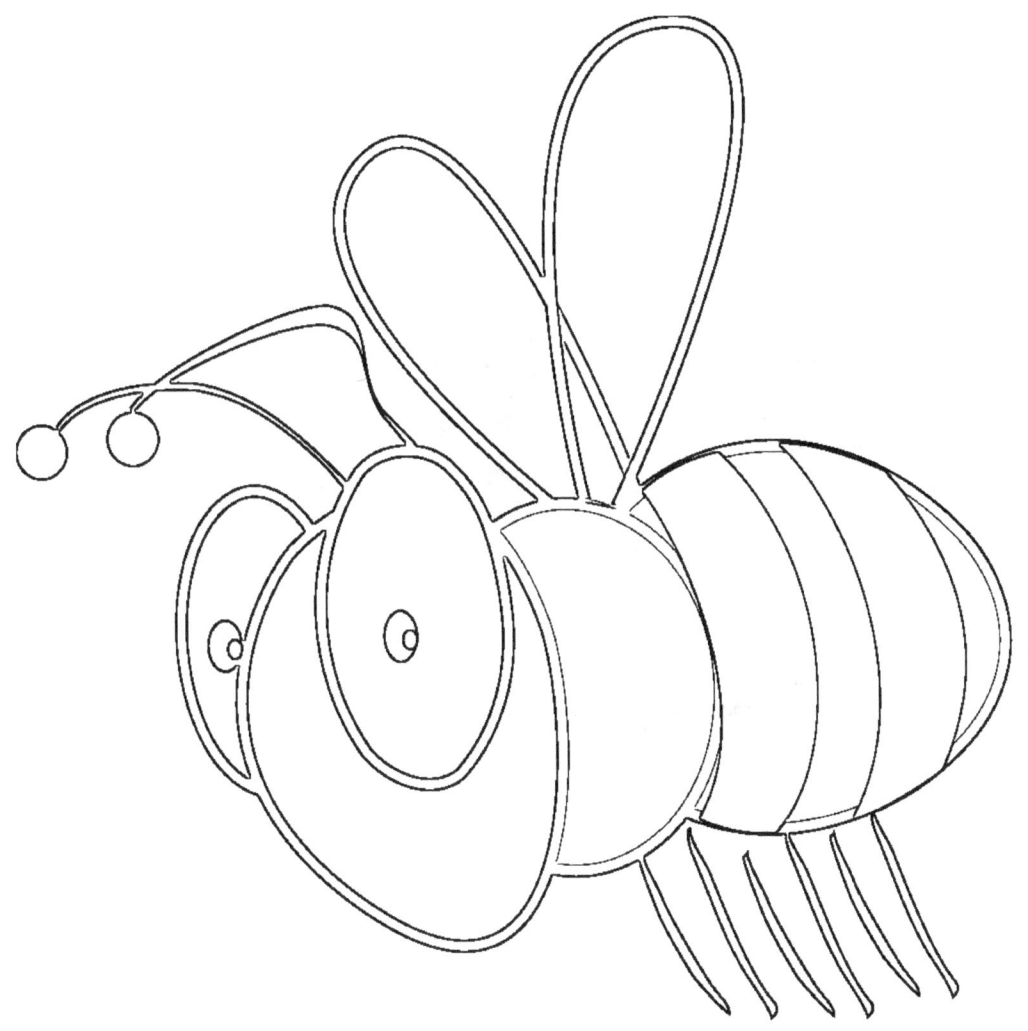

FROG

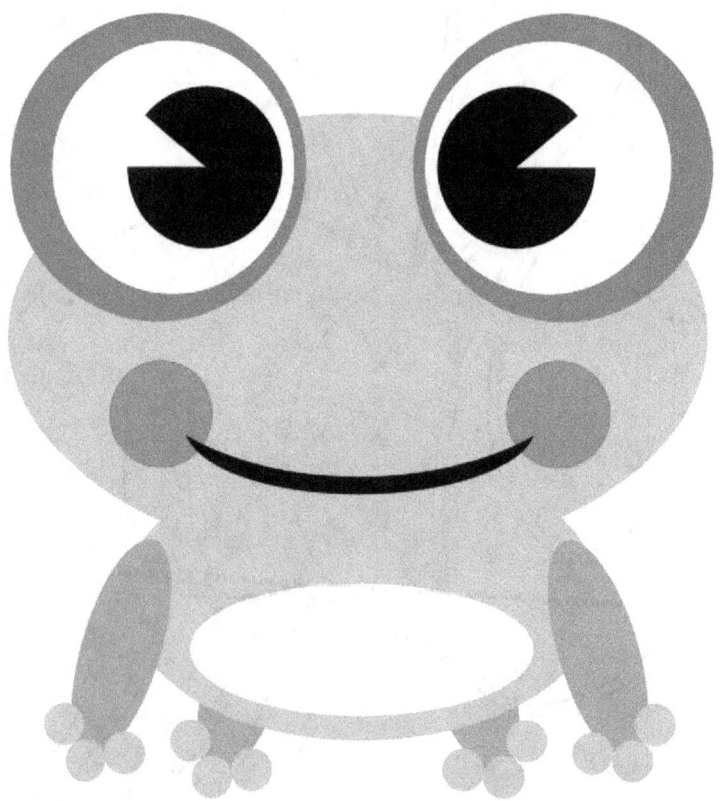

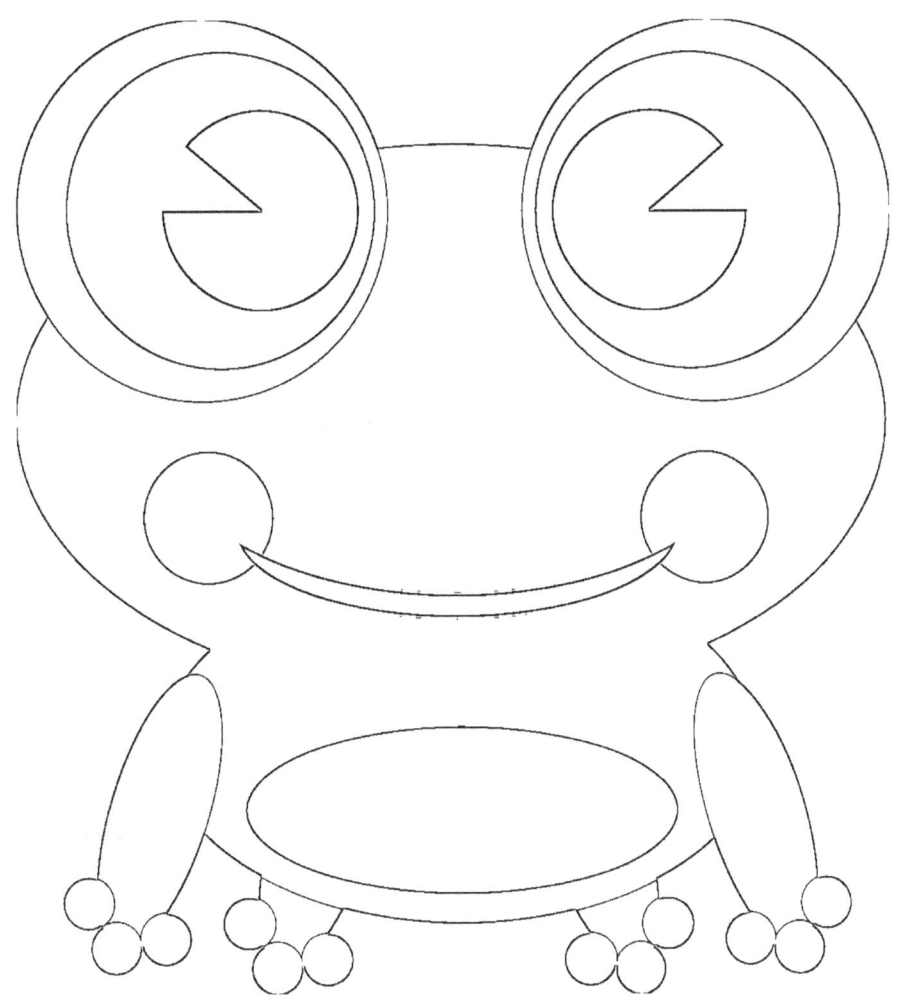

RAT

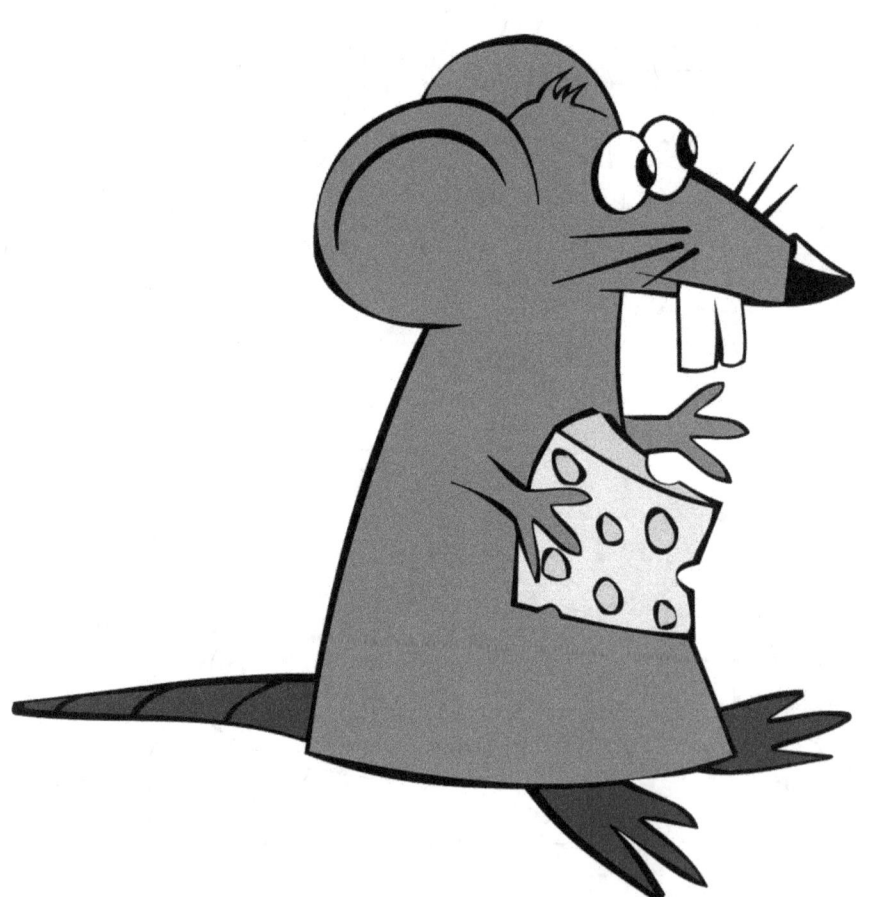

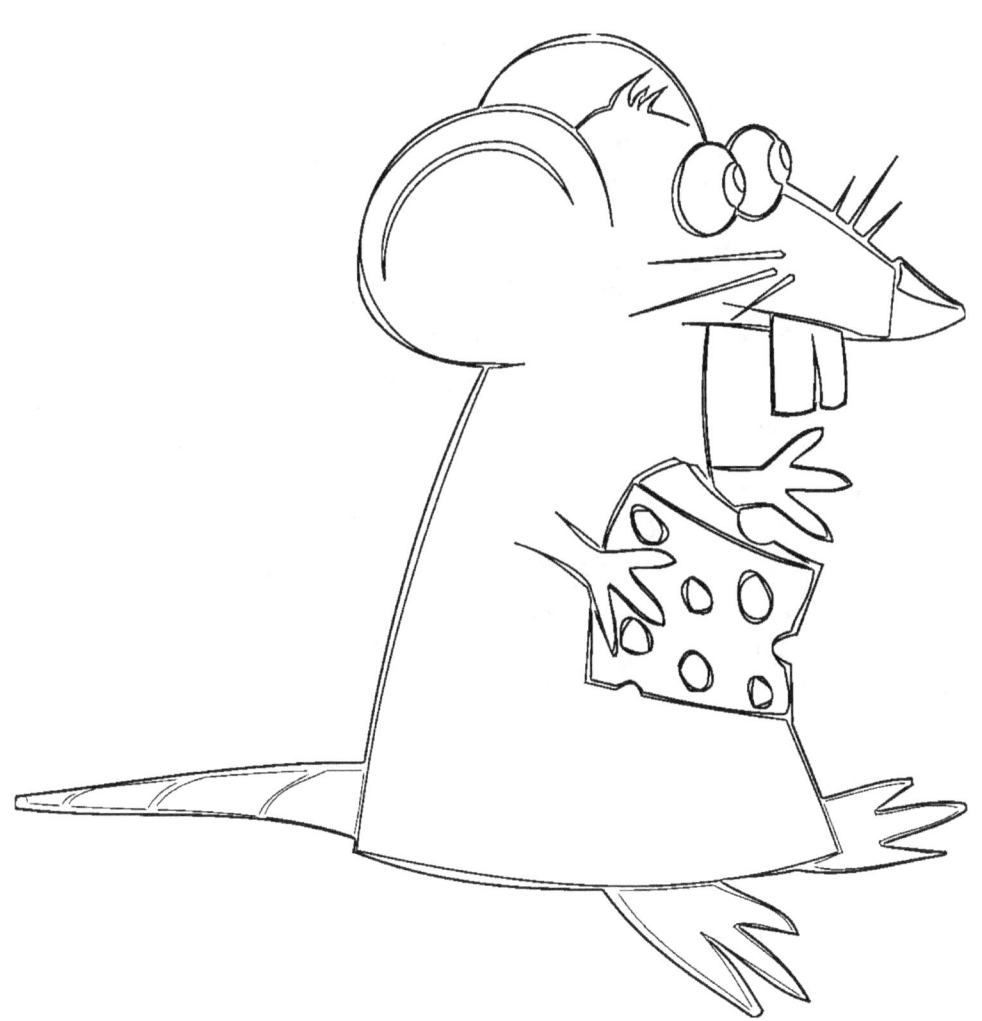

SNAIL

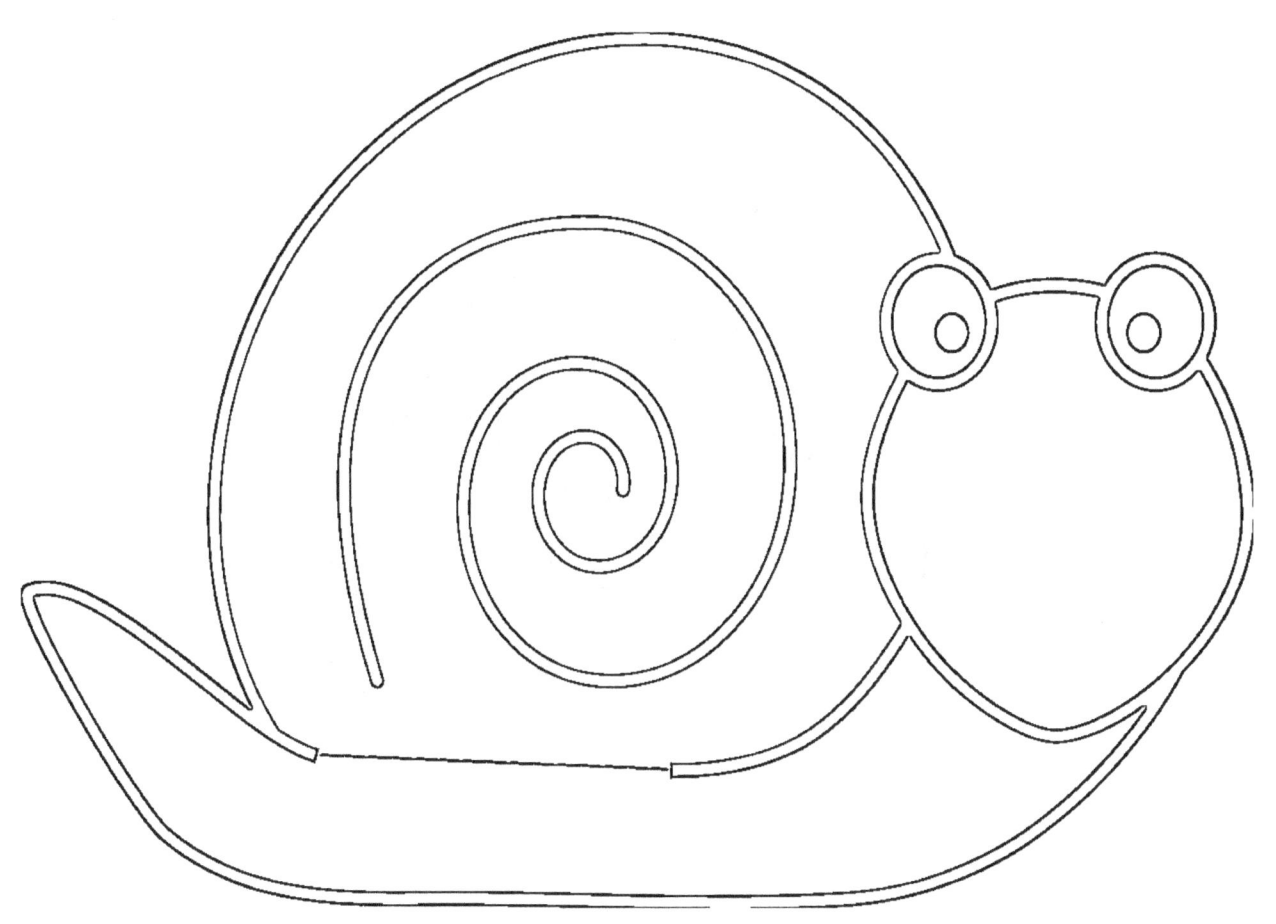

WALRUS

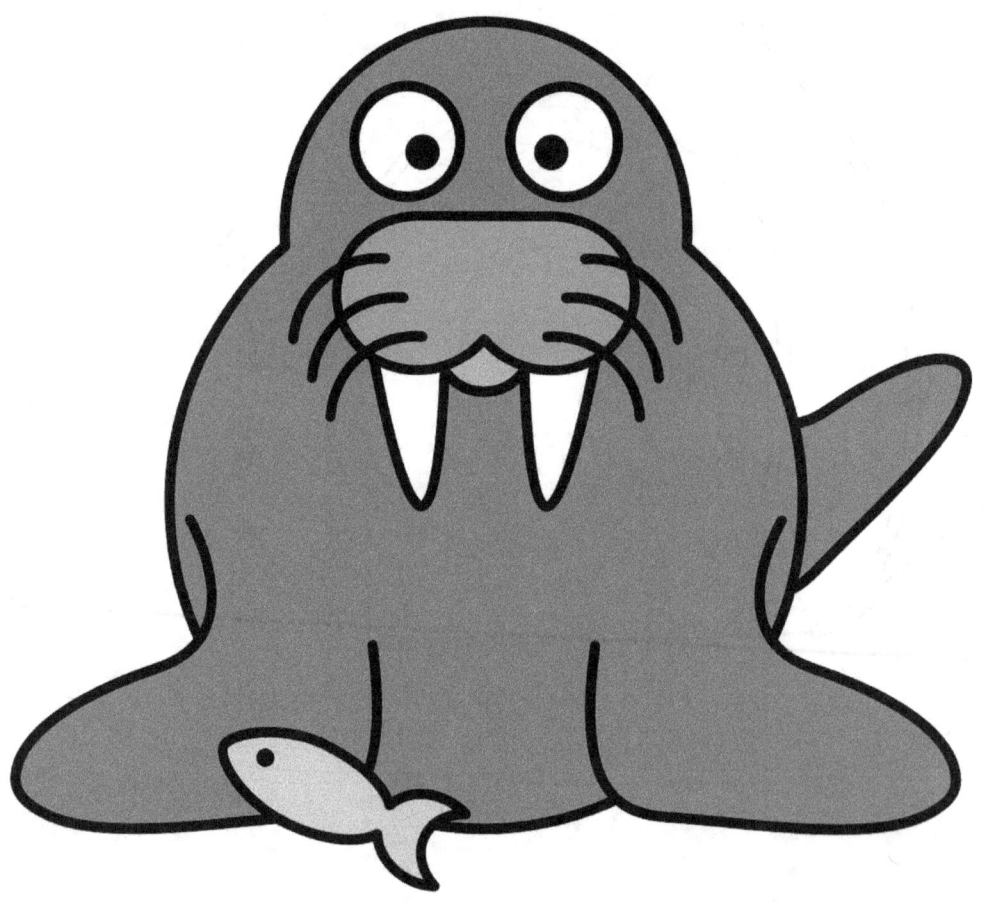

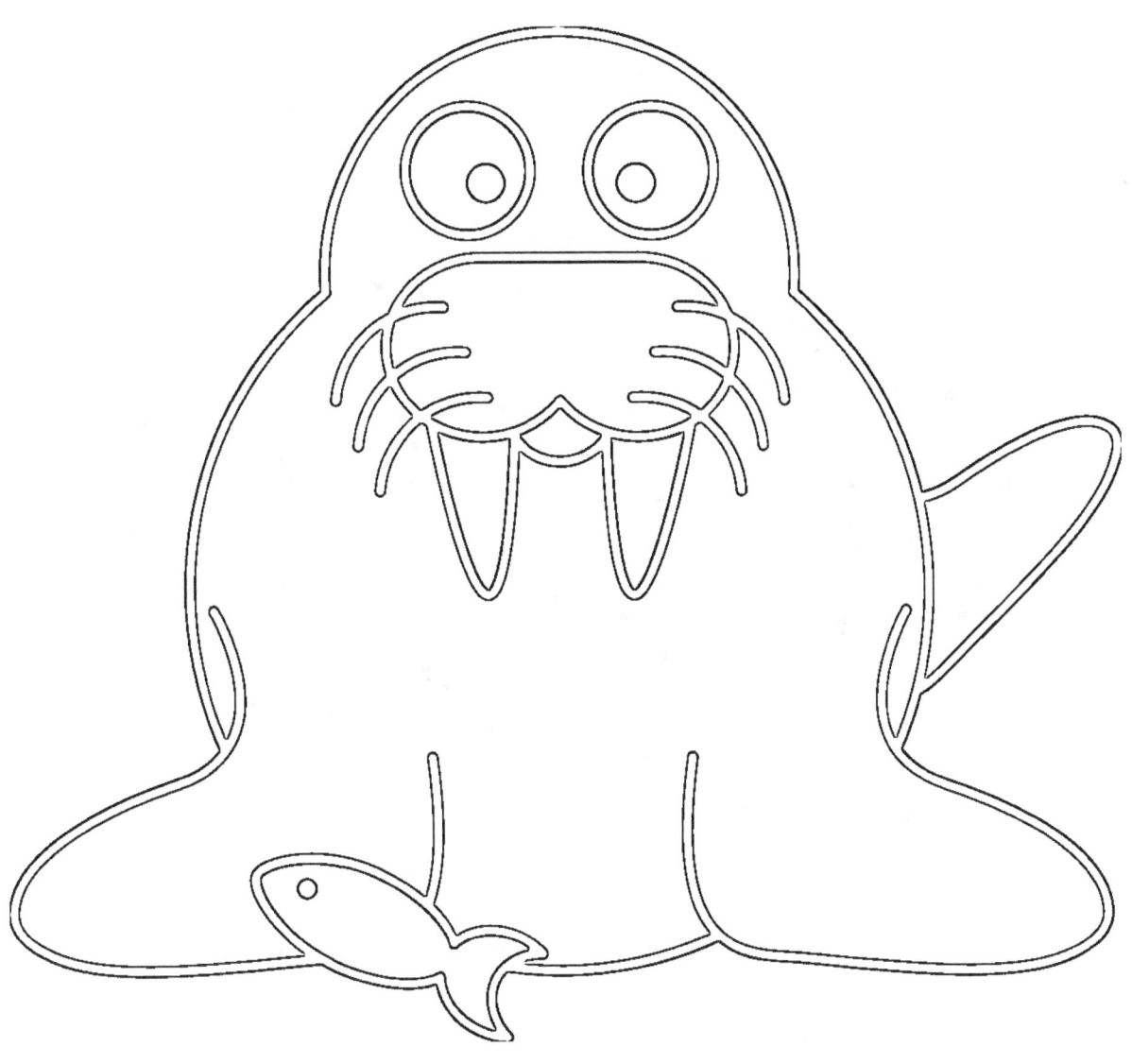

ELEPHANT

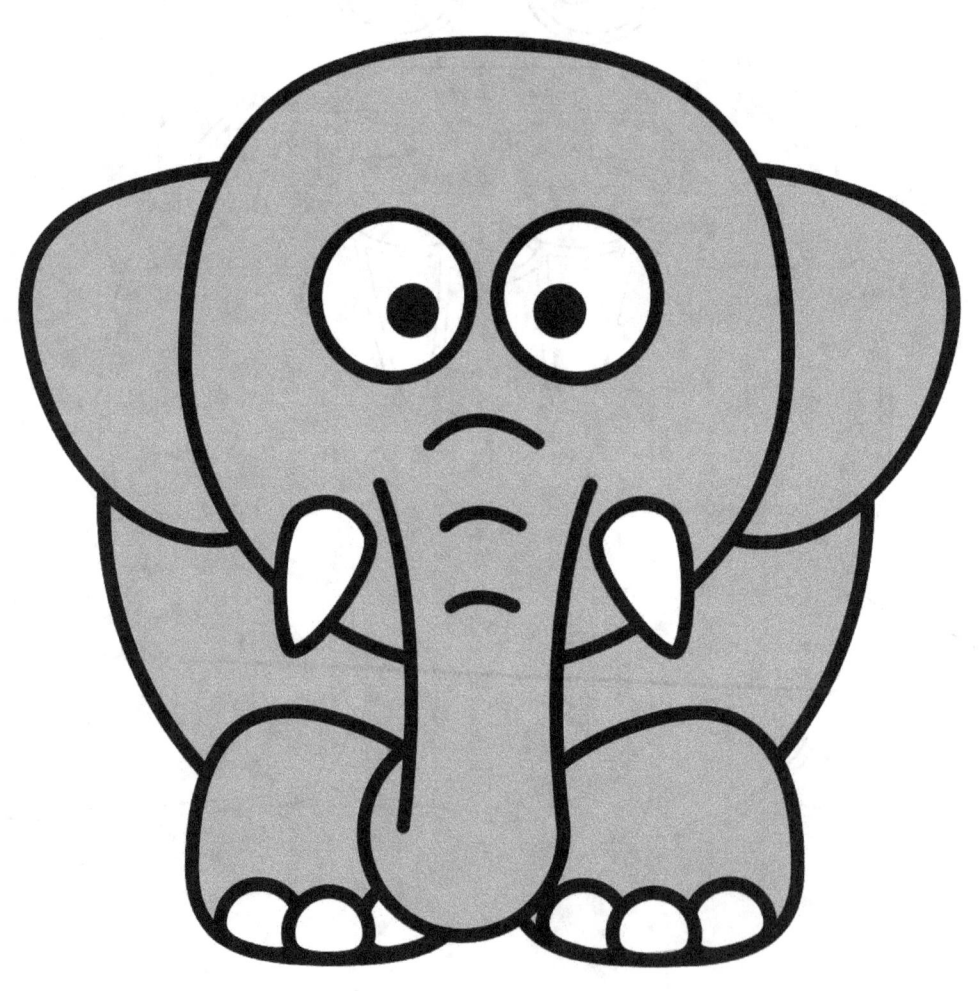

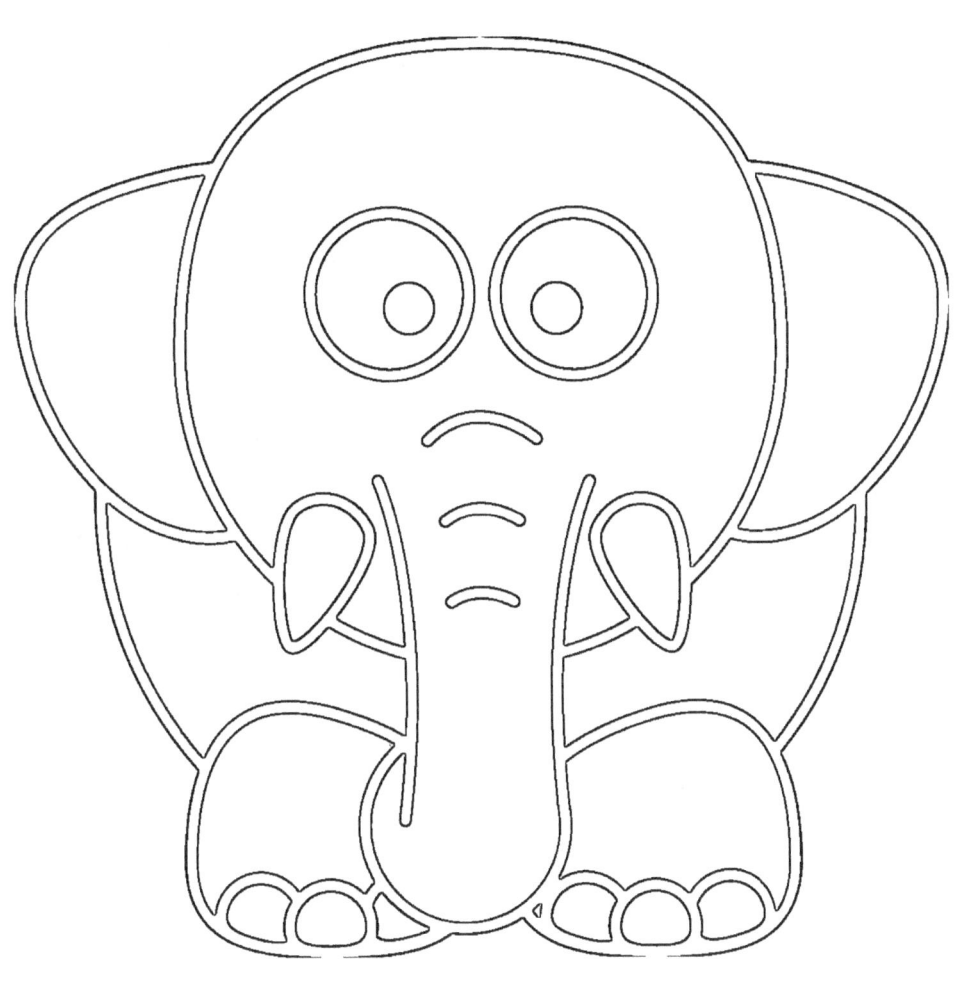

HEDGEHOG

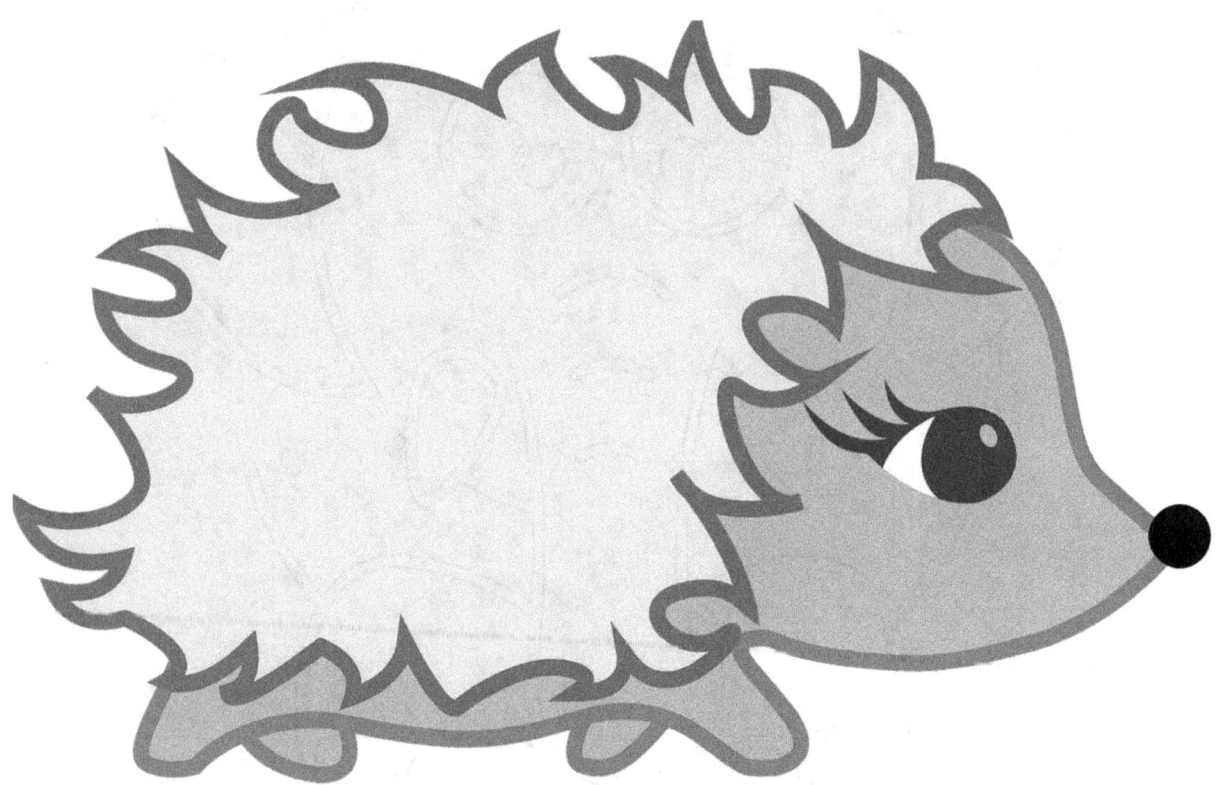

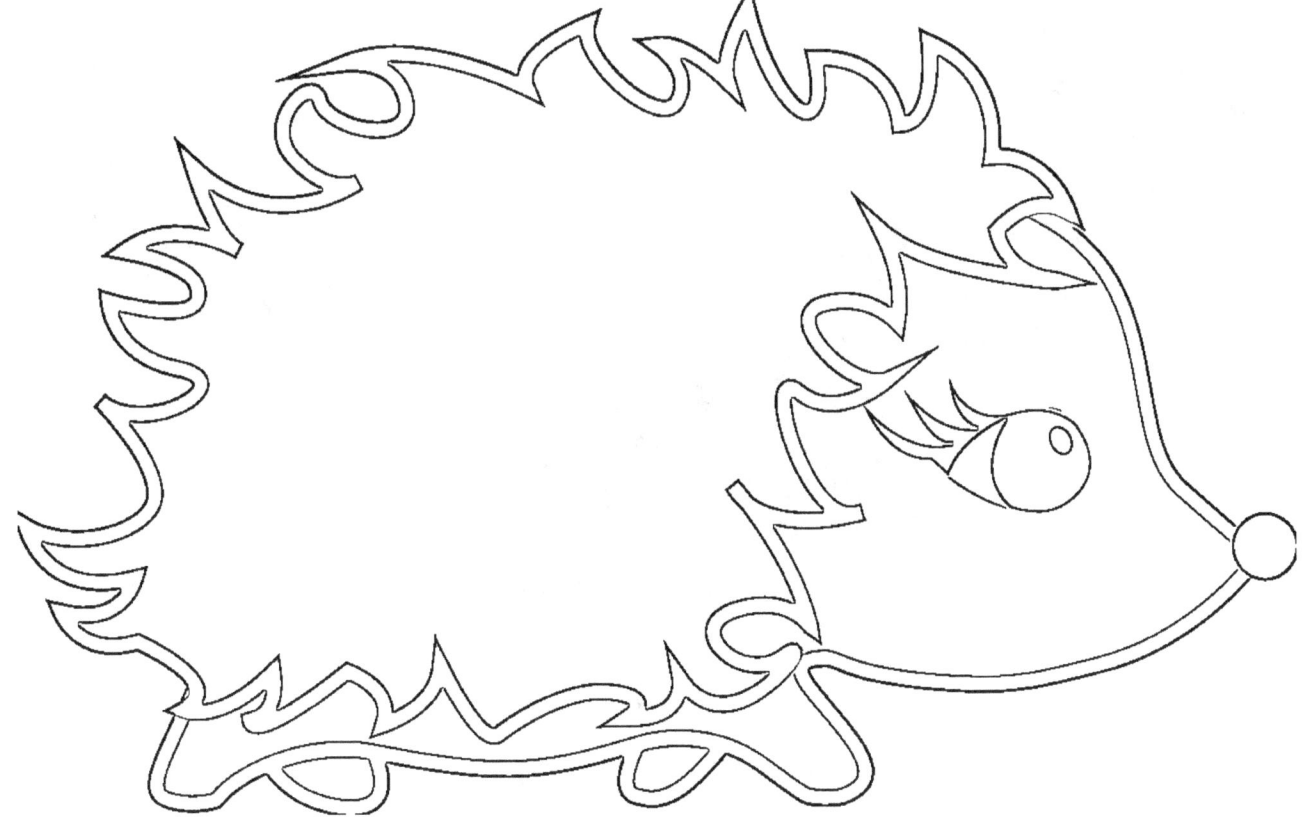

ELK

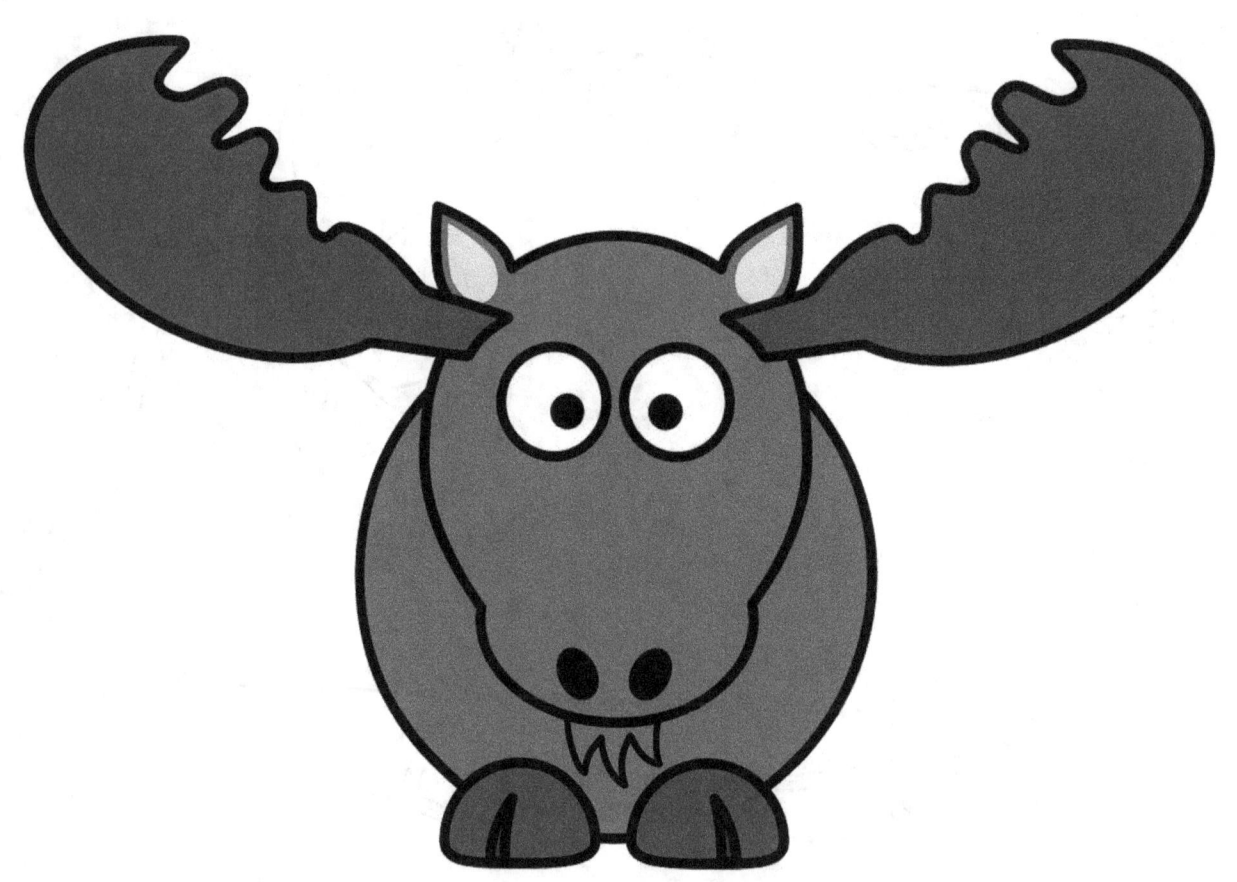

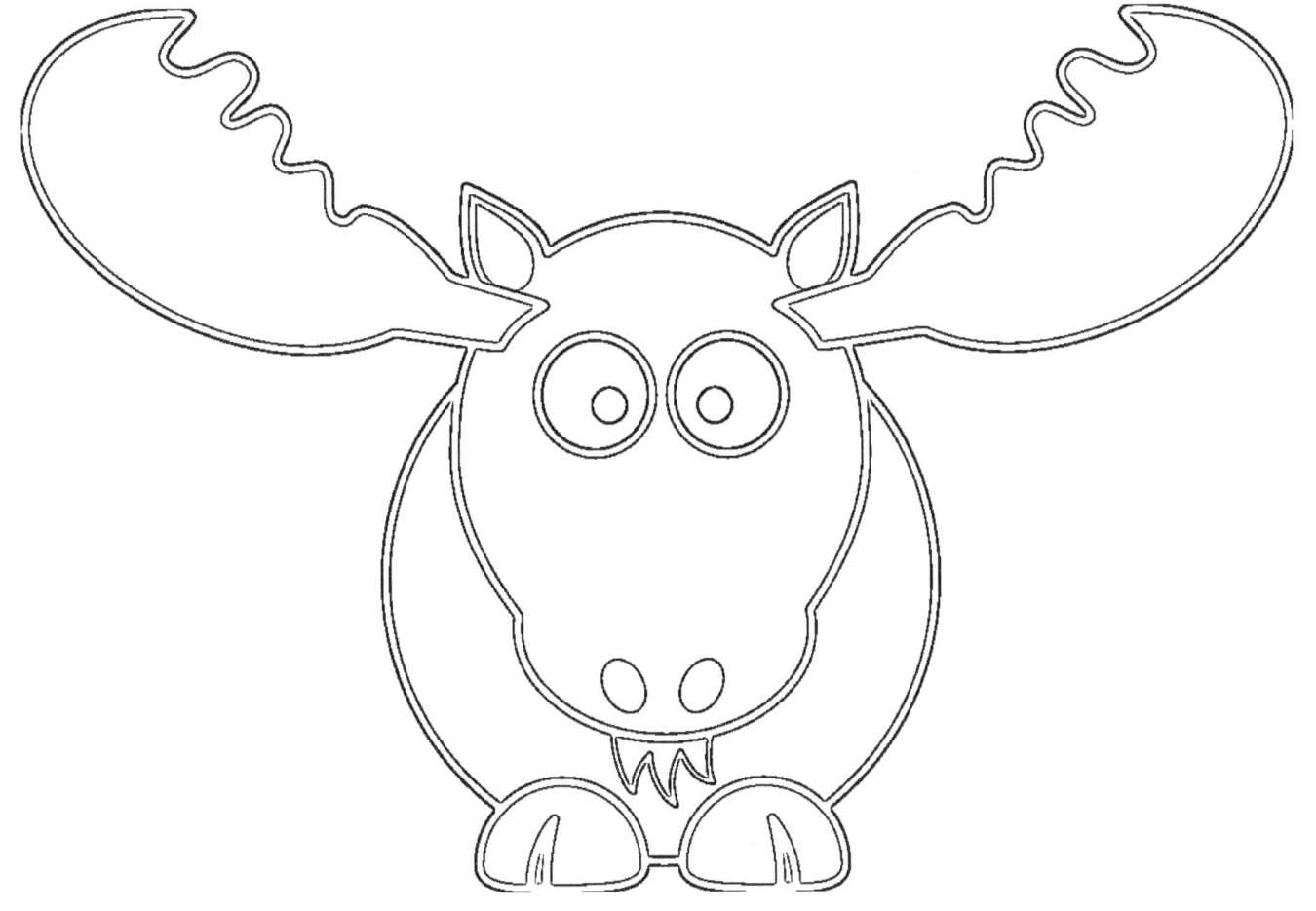

GAZELLE

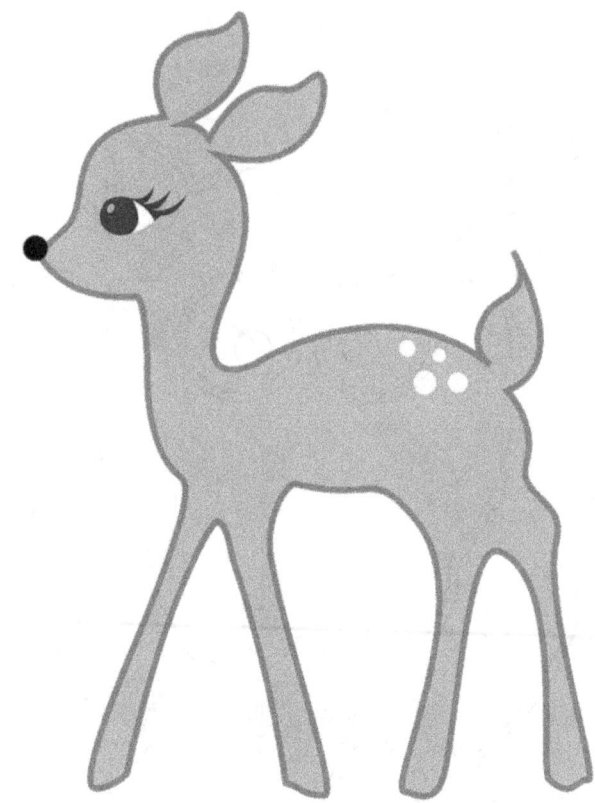

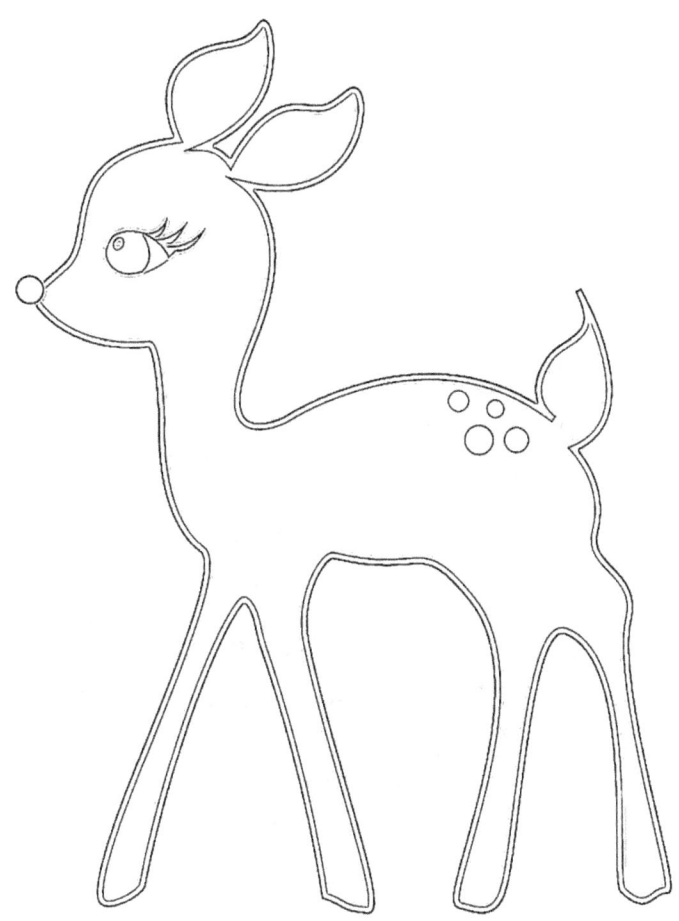

CAT

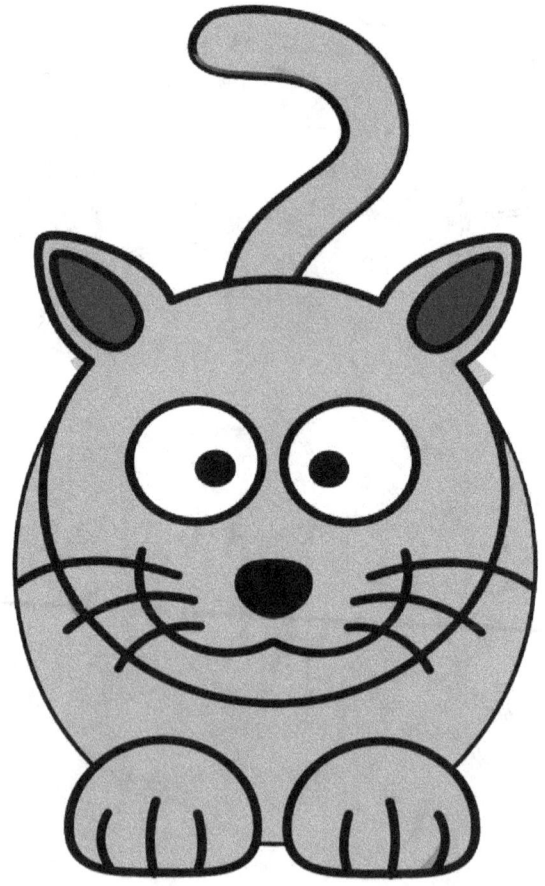

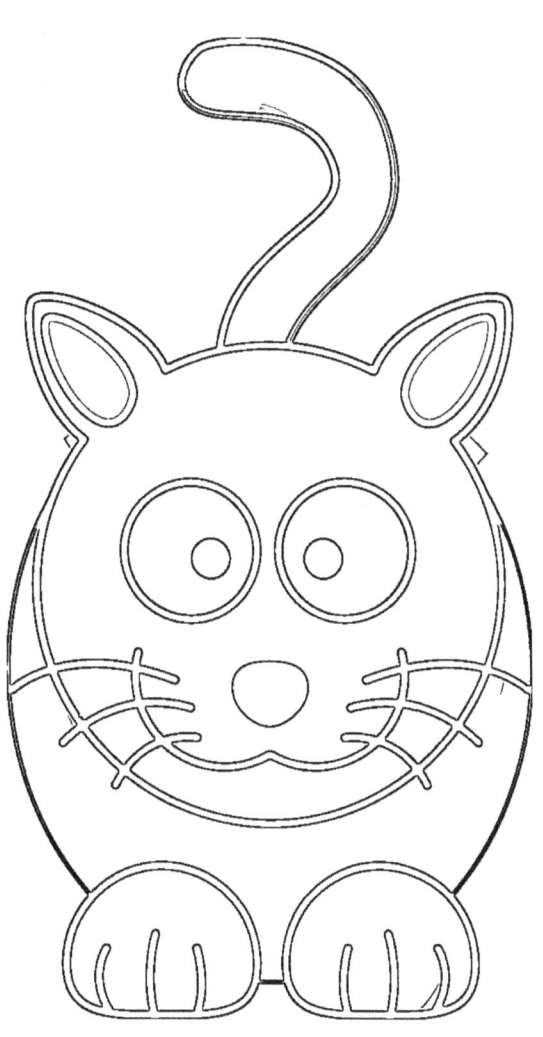

HIPPOPOTAMUS

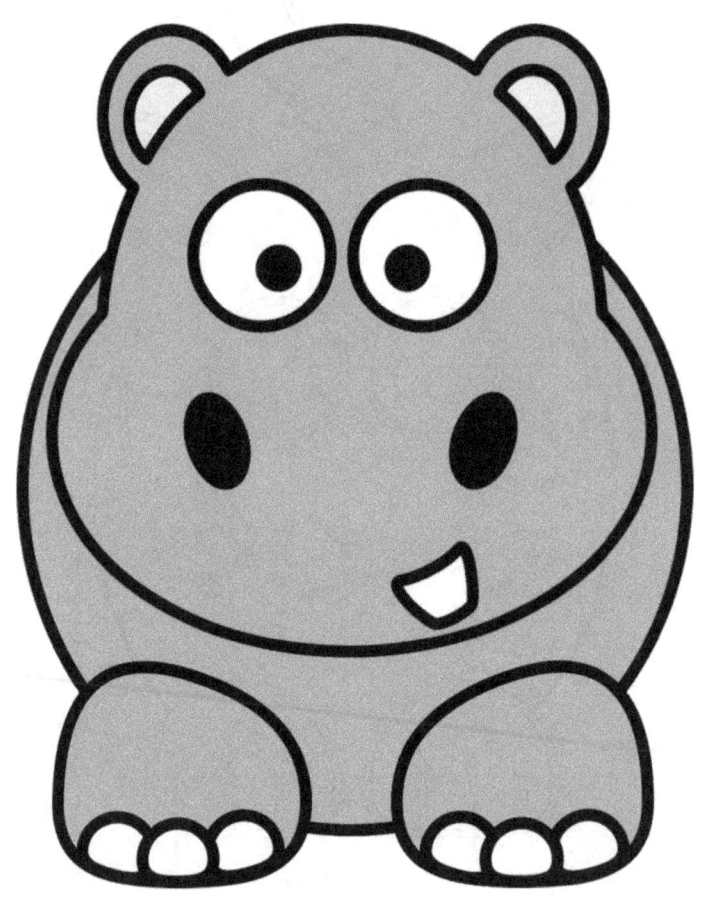

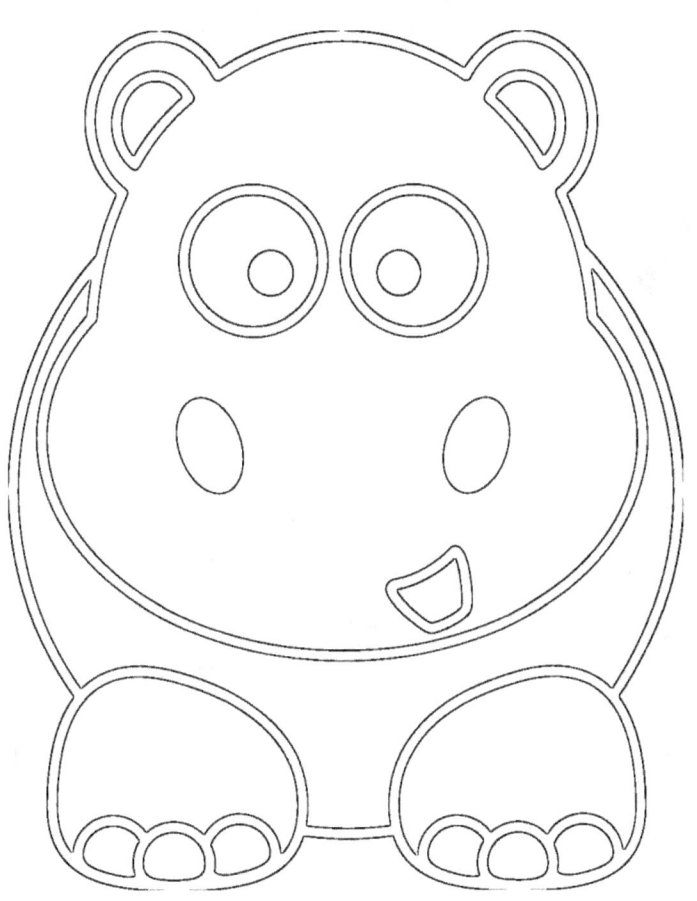

SNAKE

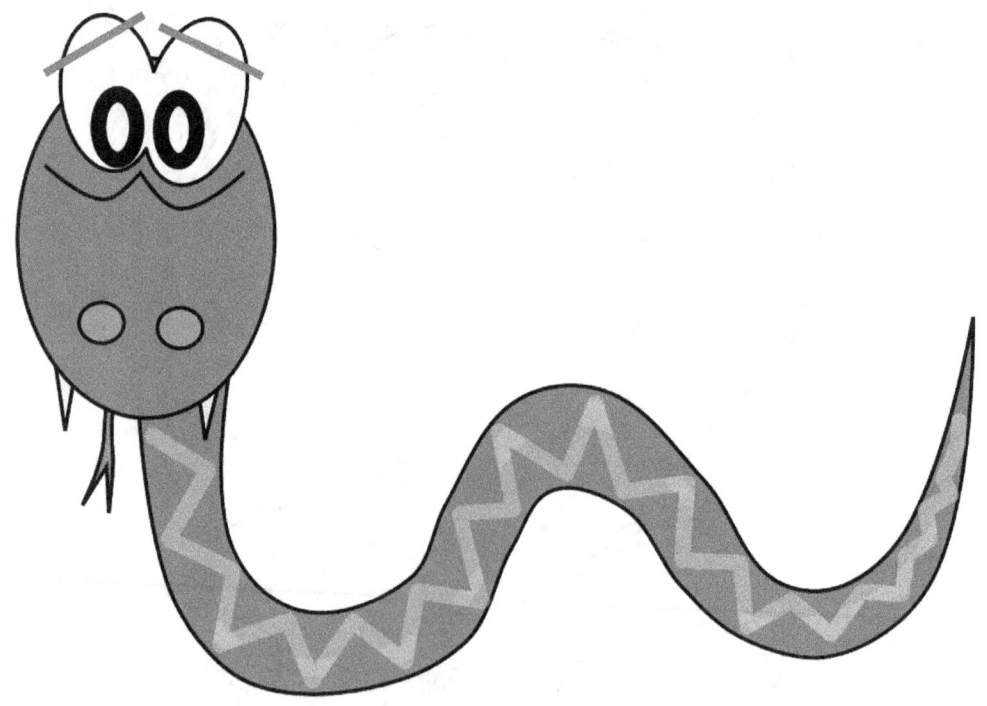

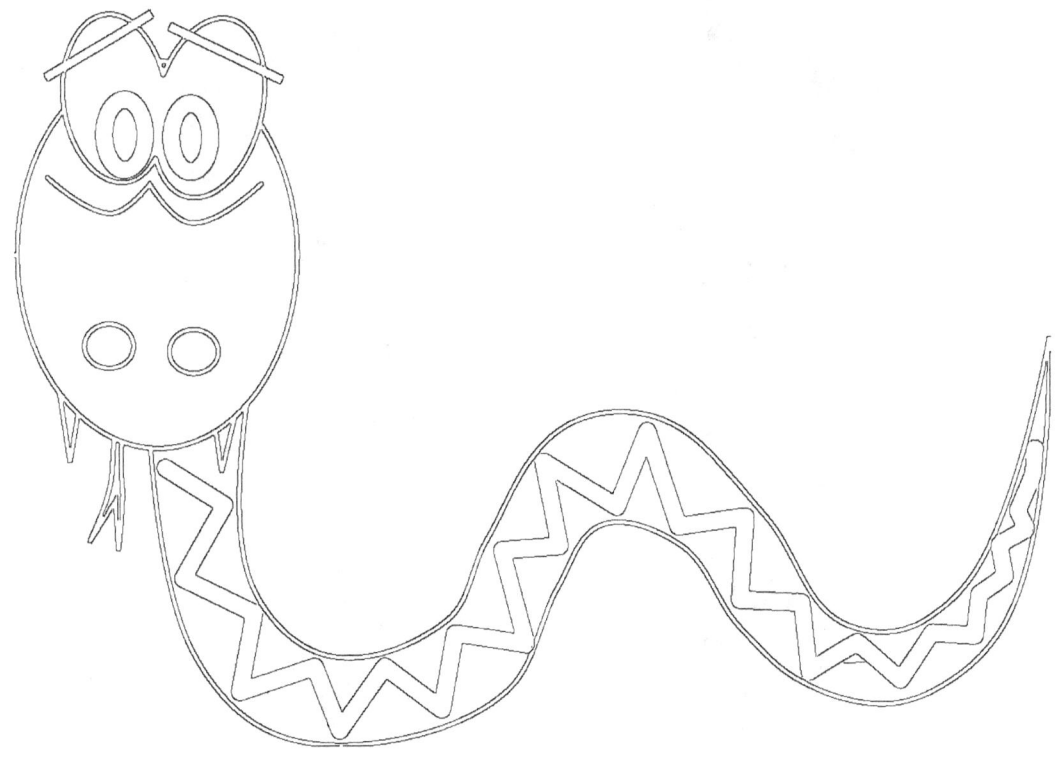

PANDA

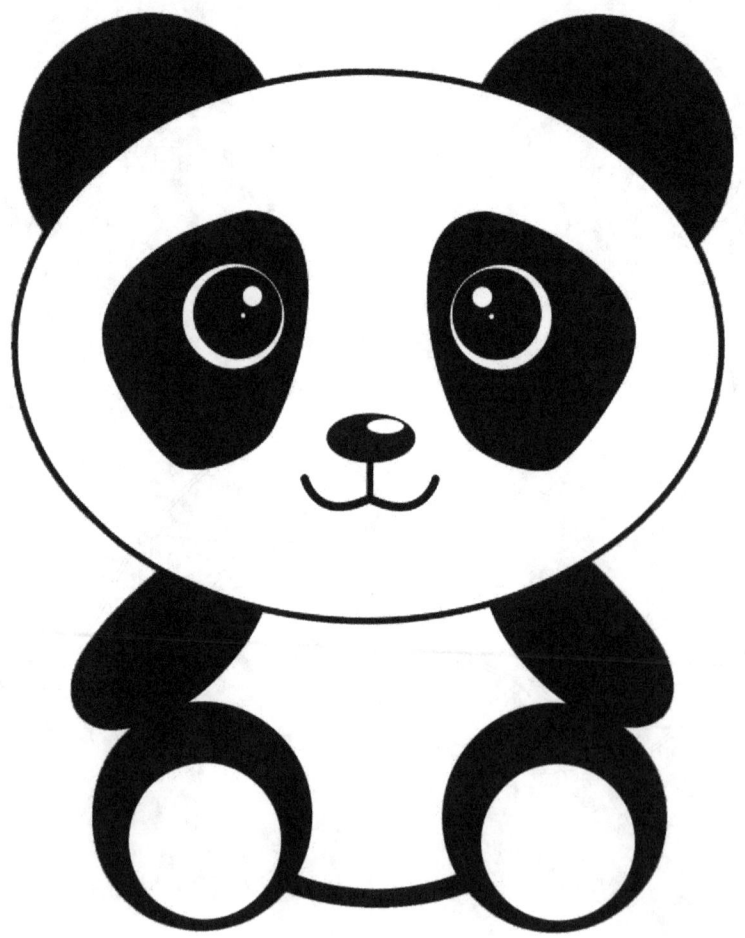

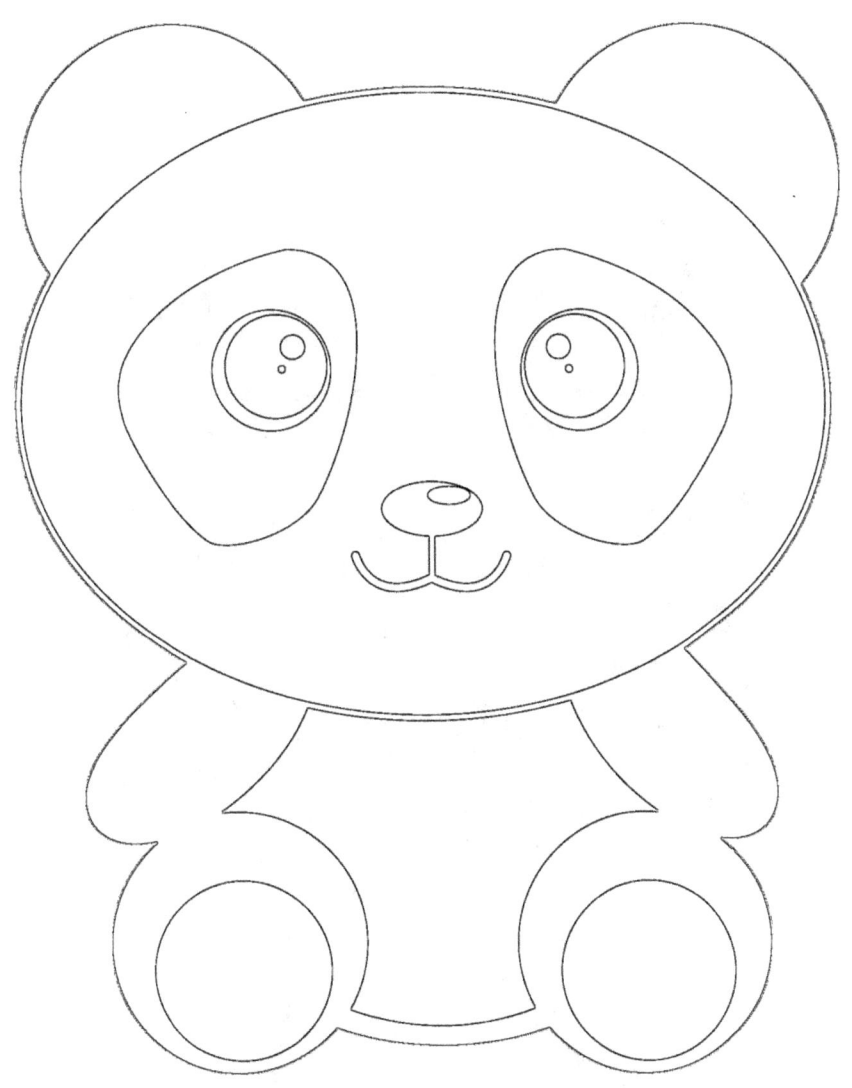

OX

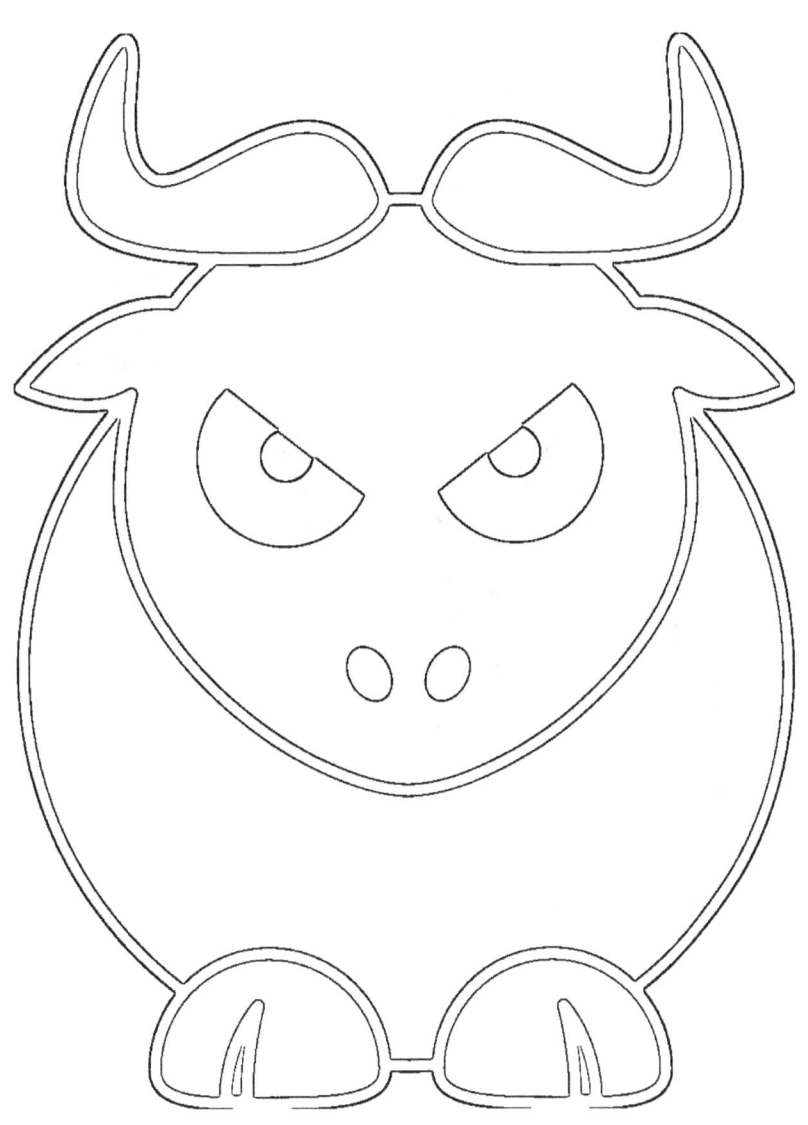

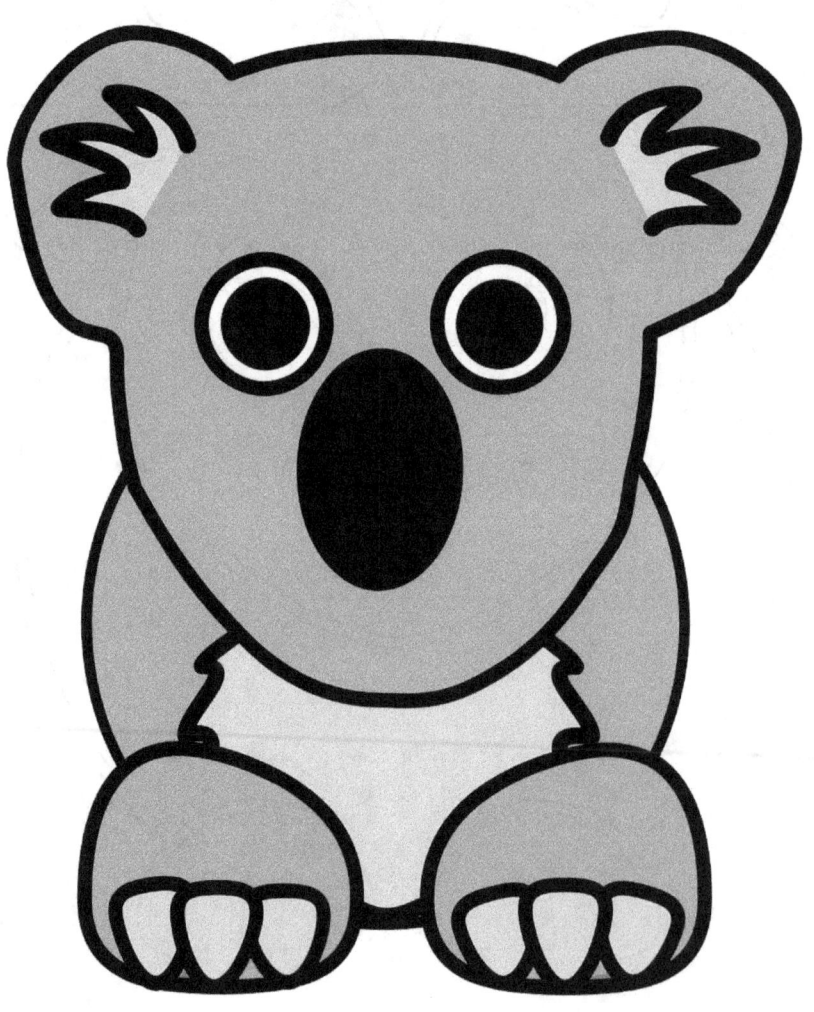

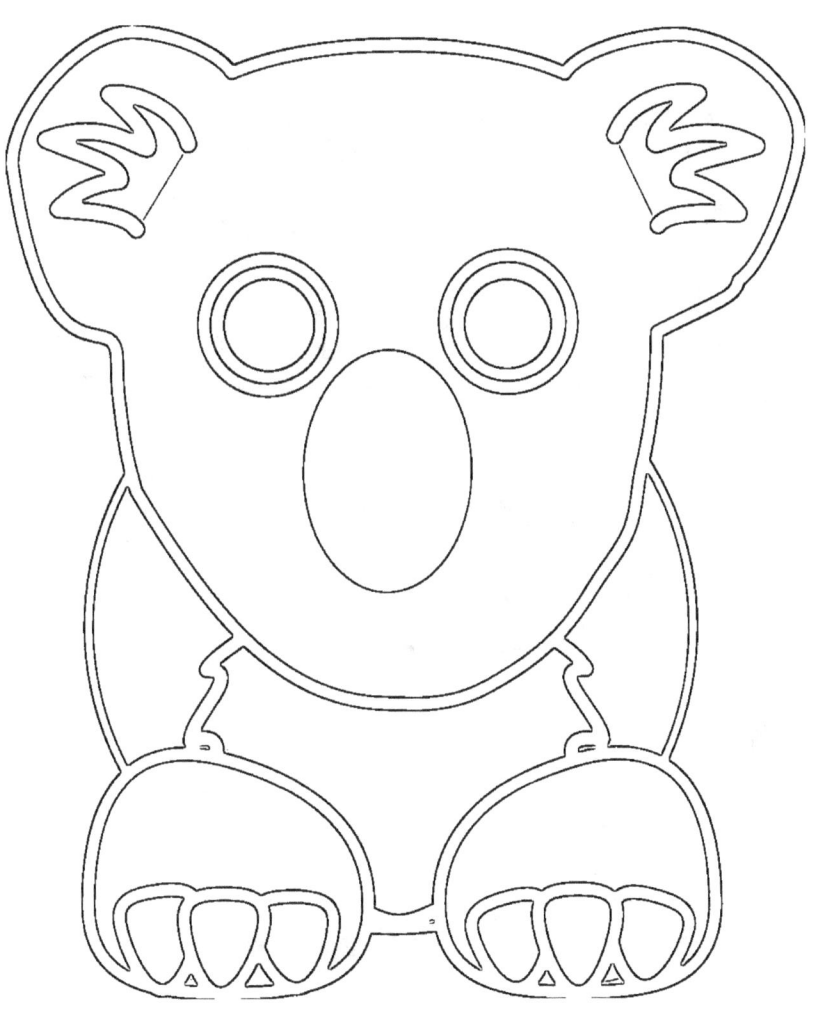

PIG

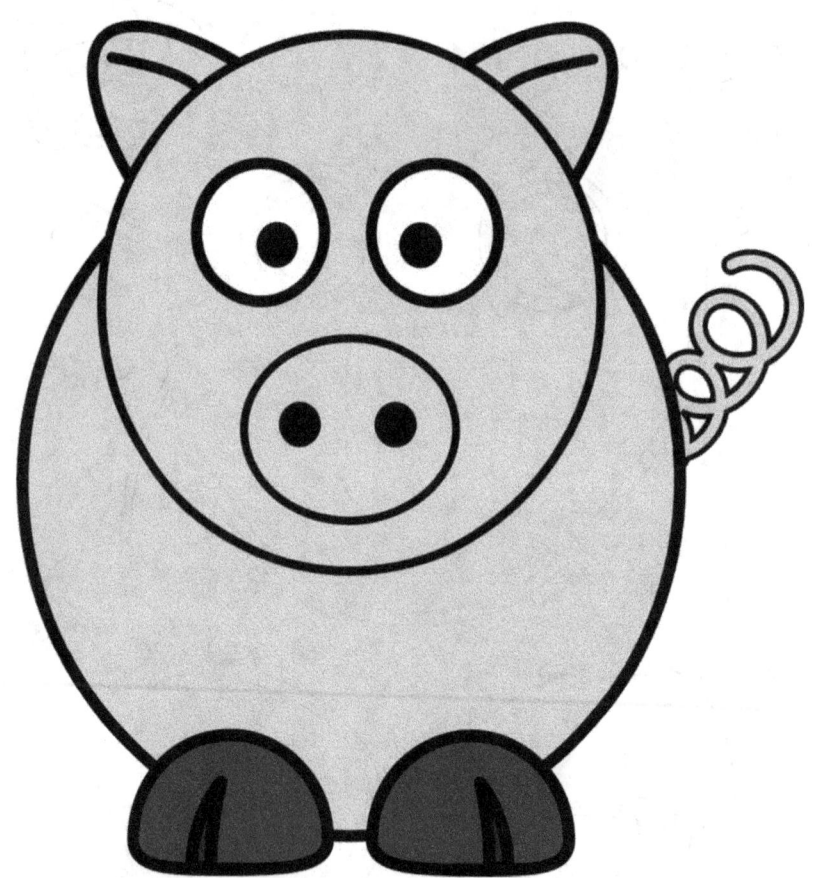

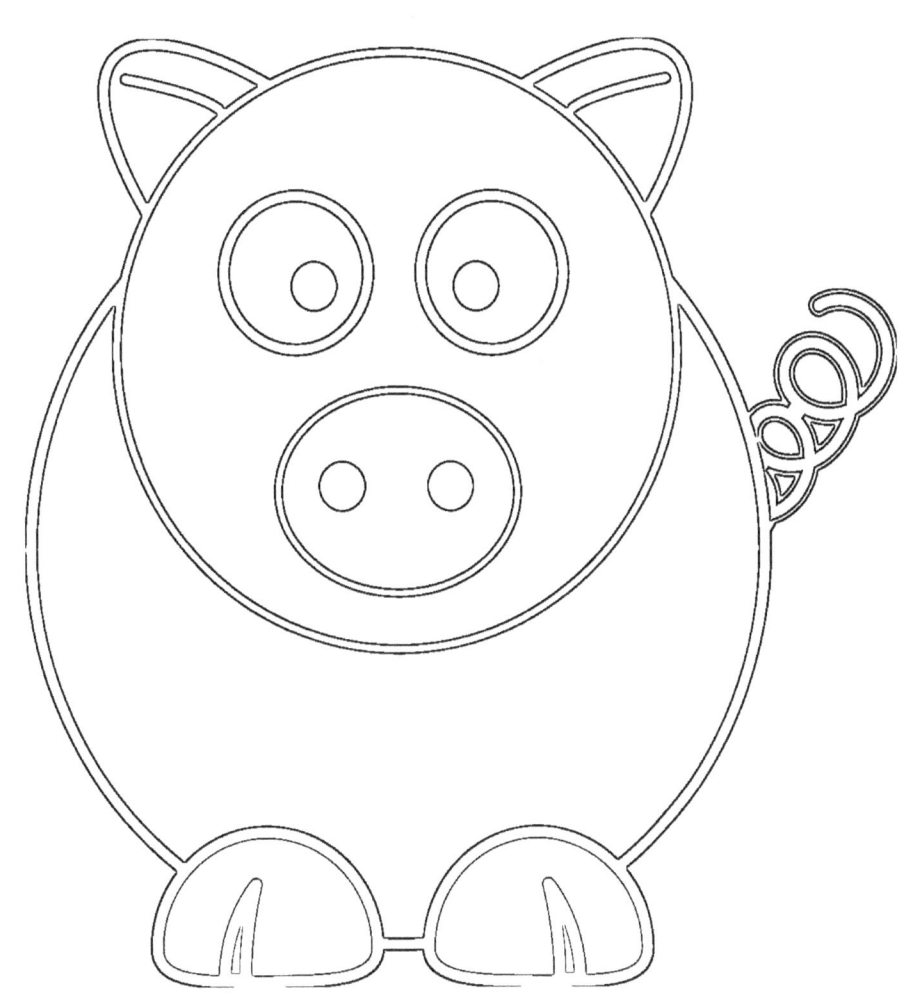

FOX

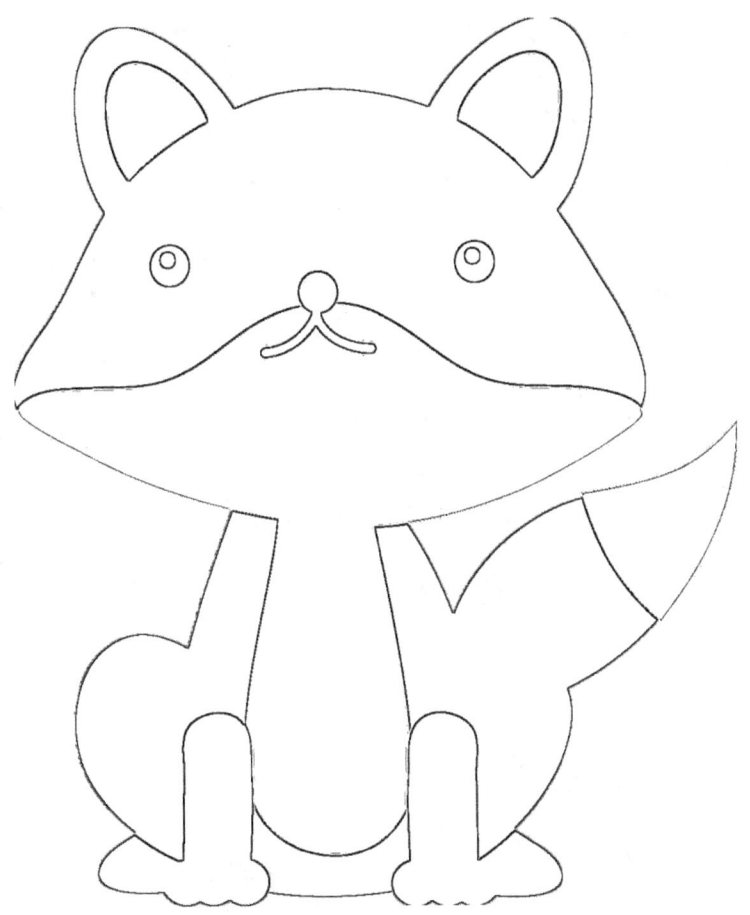

COW

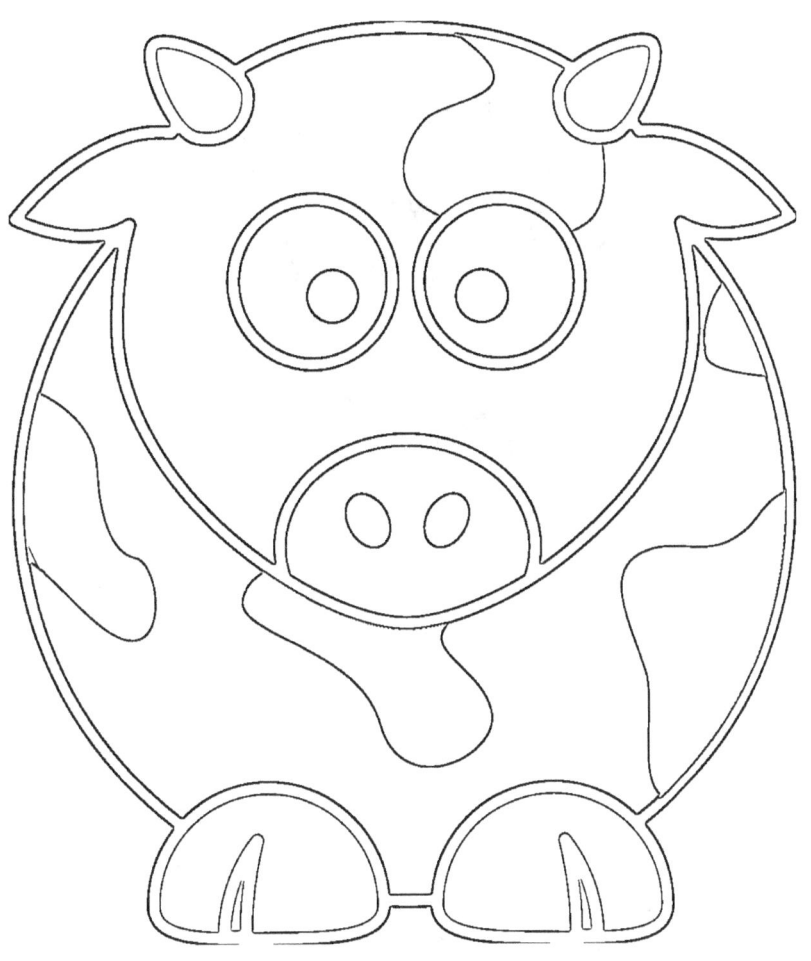

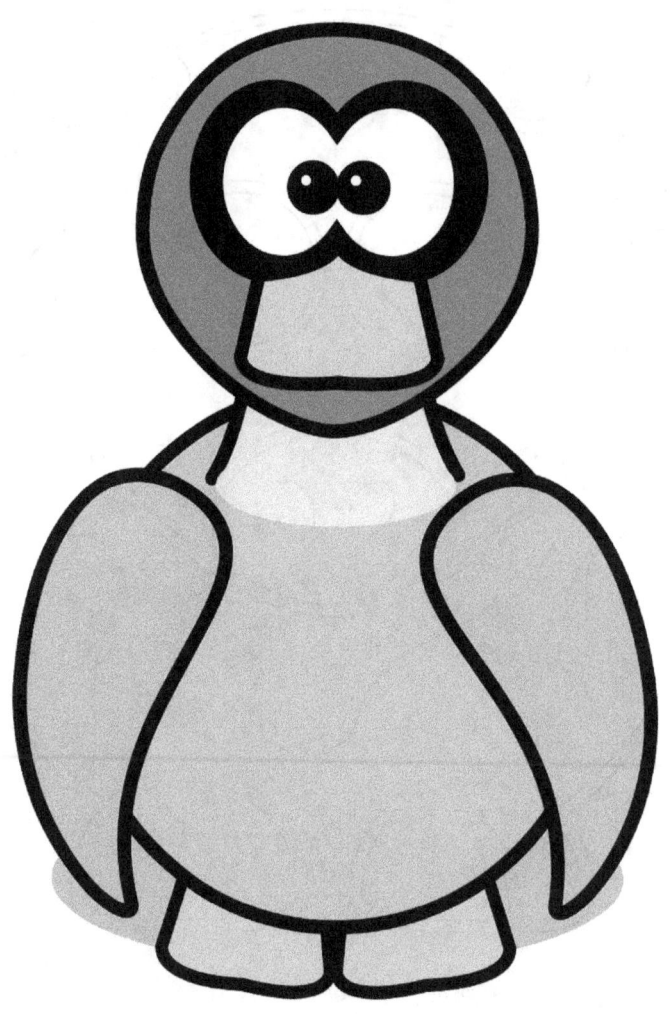

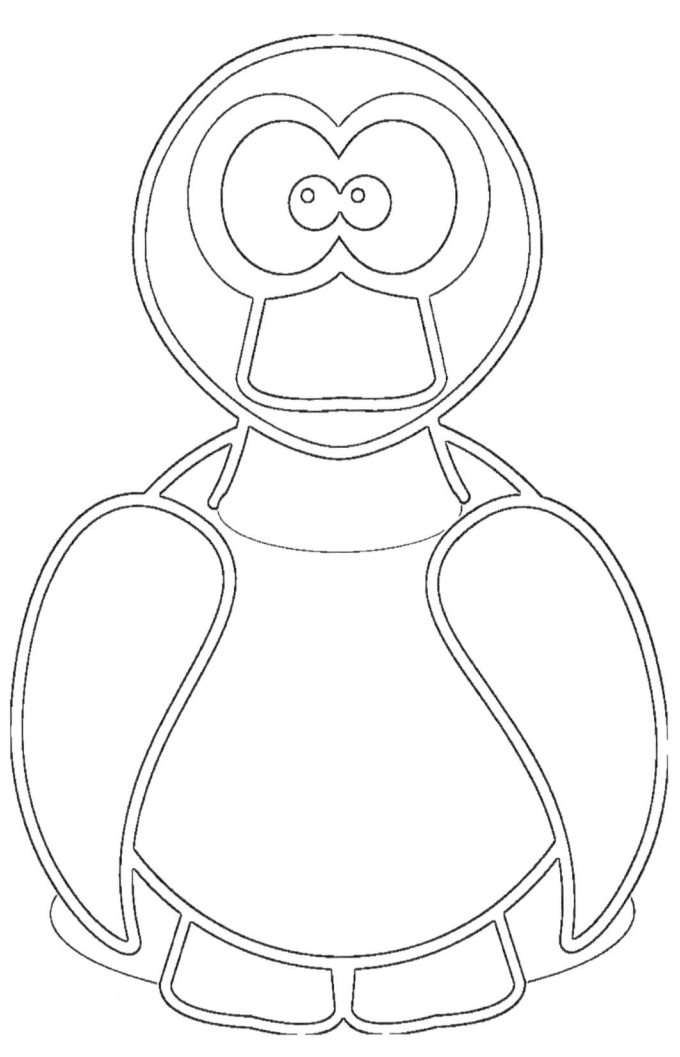

OWL

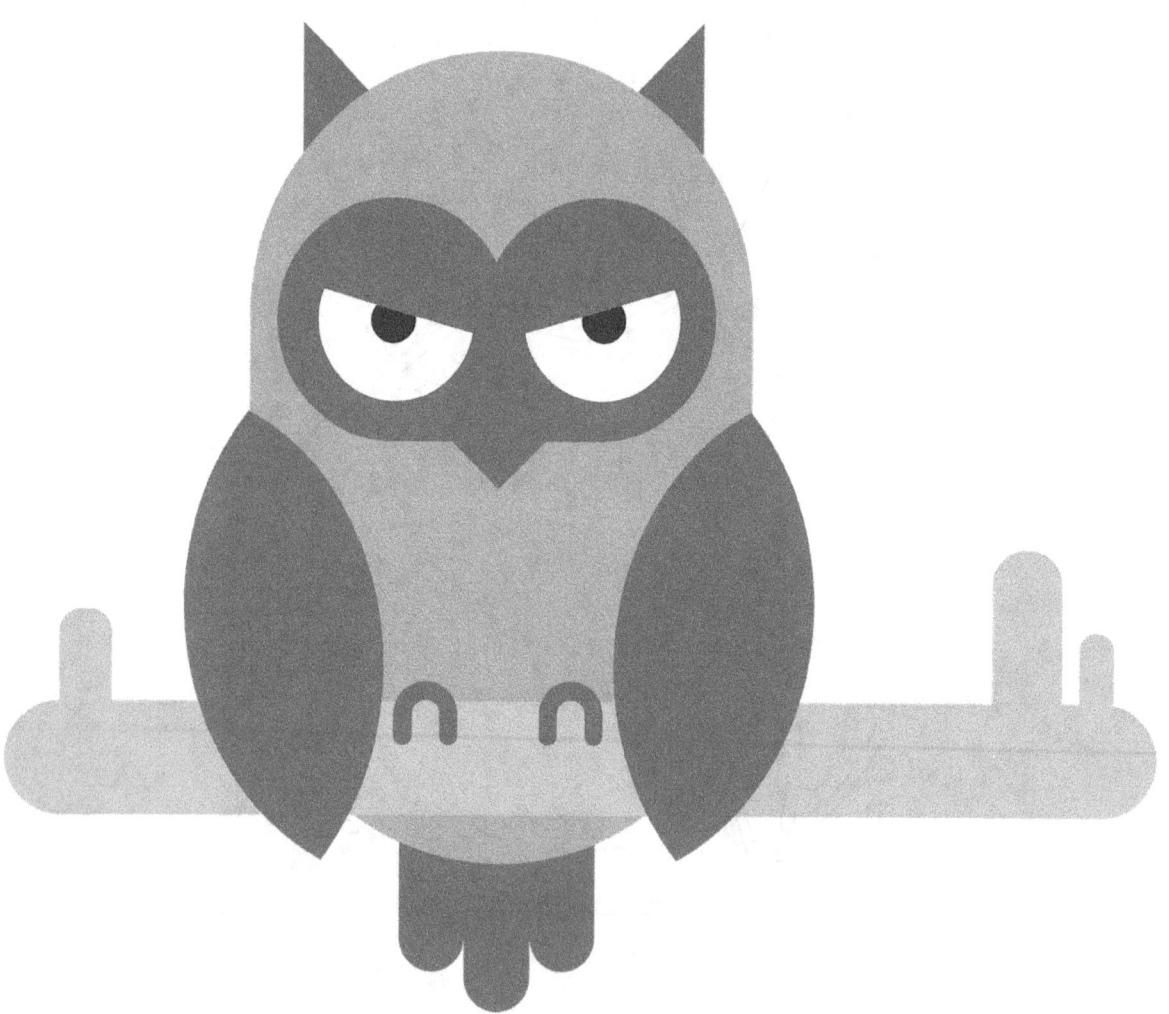

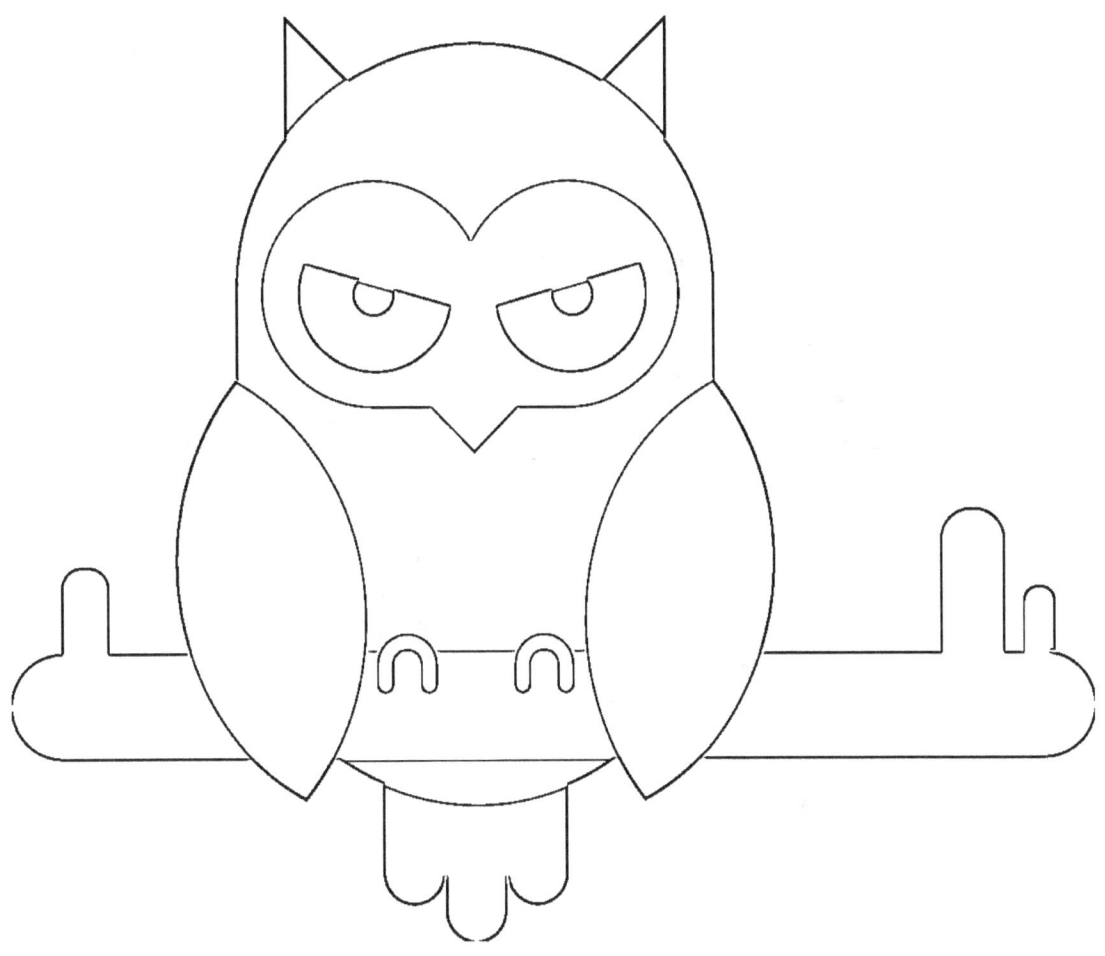

SHEEP

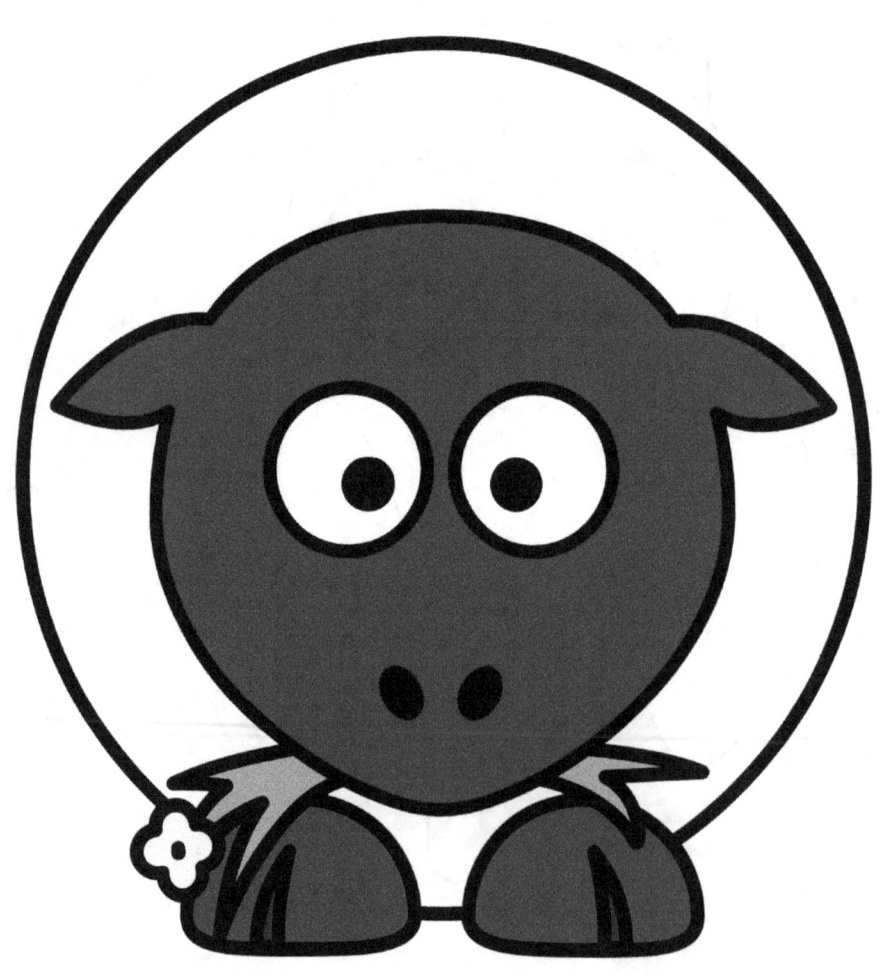

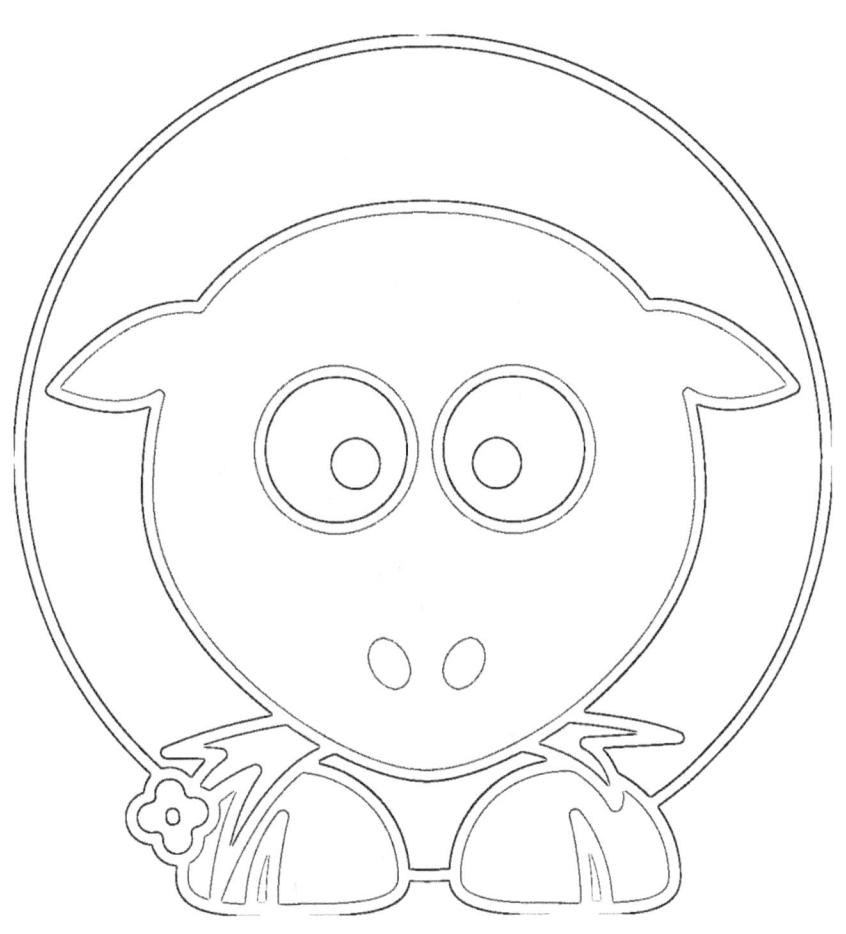

DOG

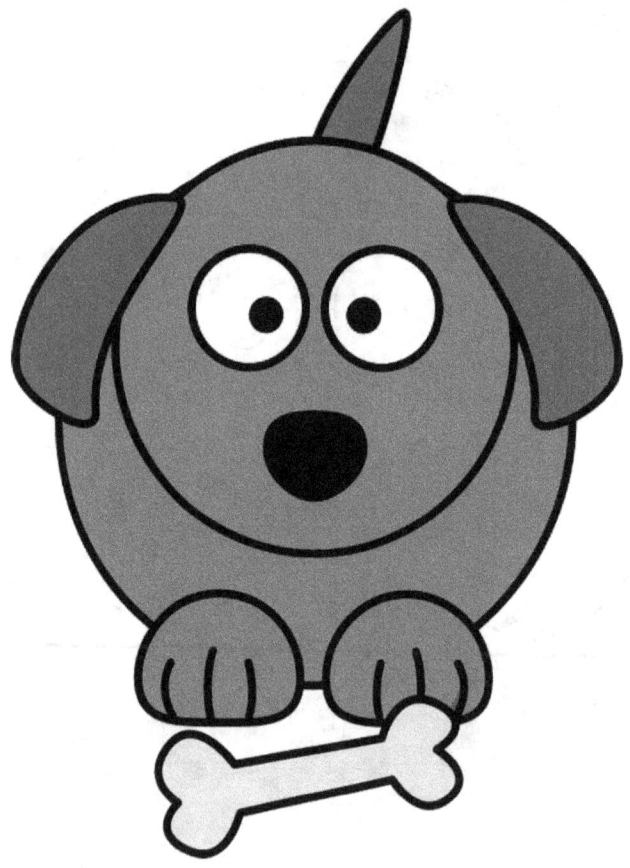

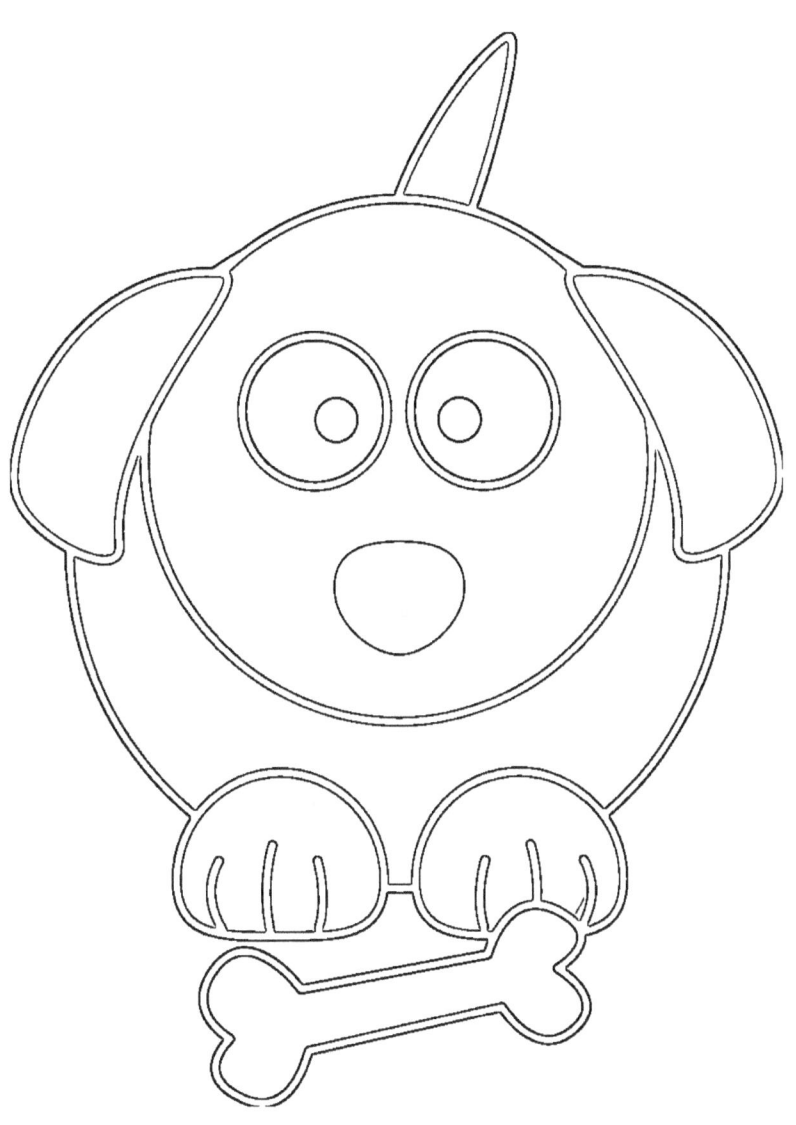

BEAR

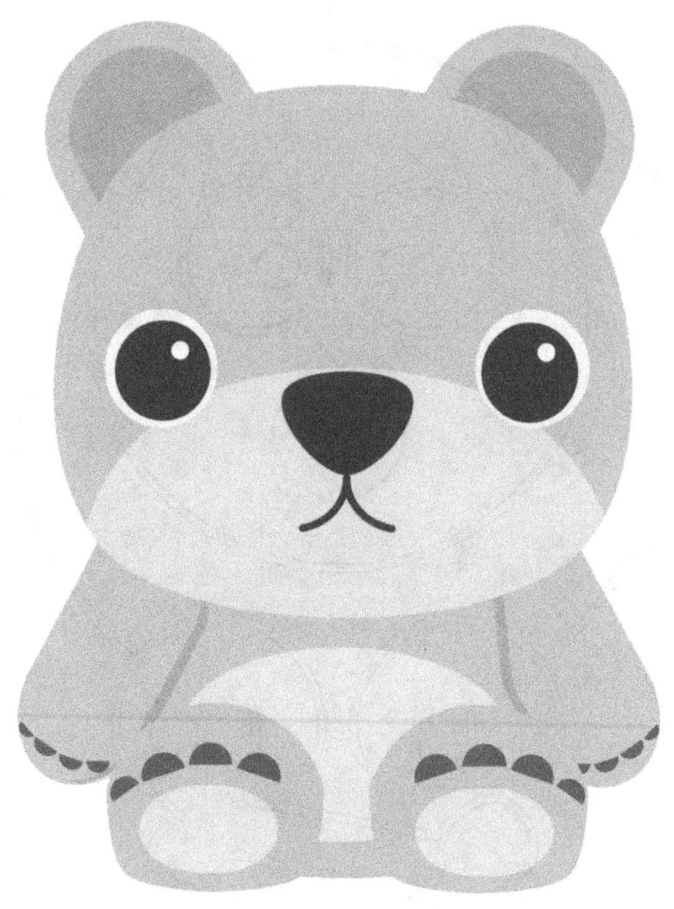

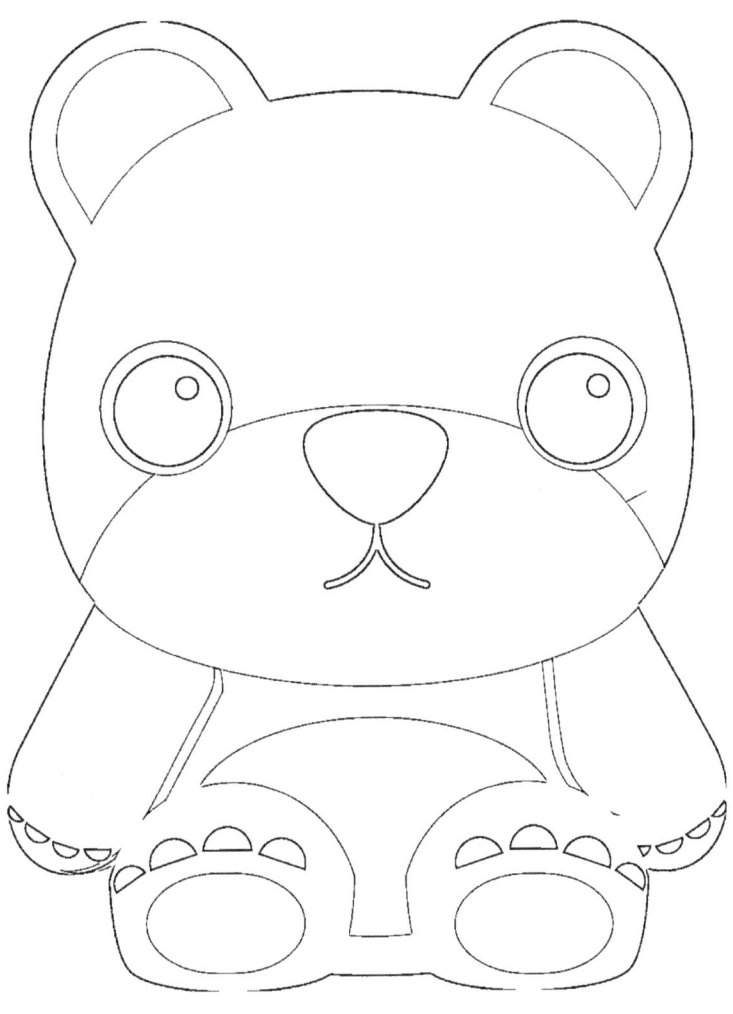

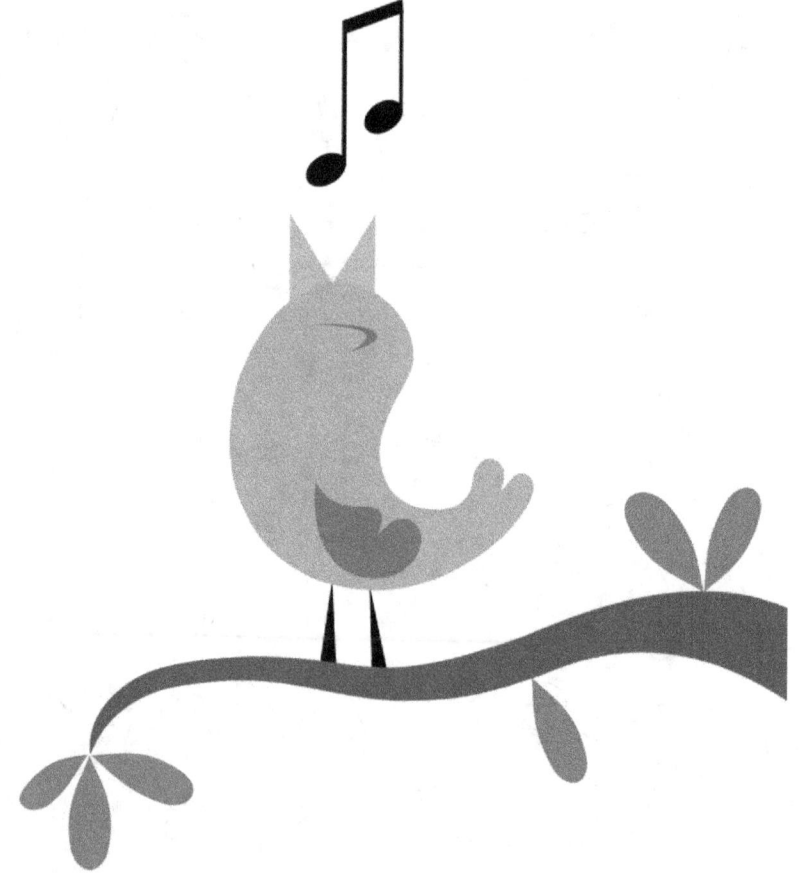

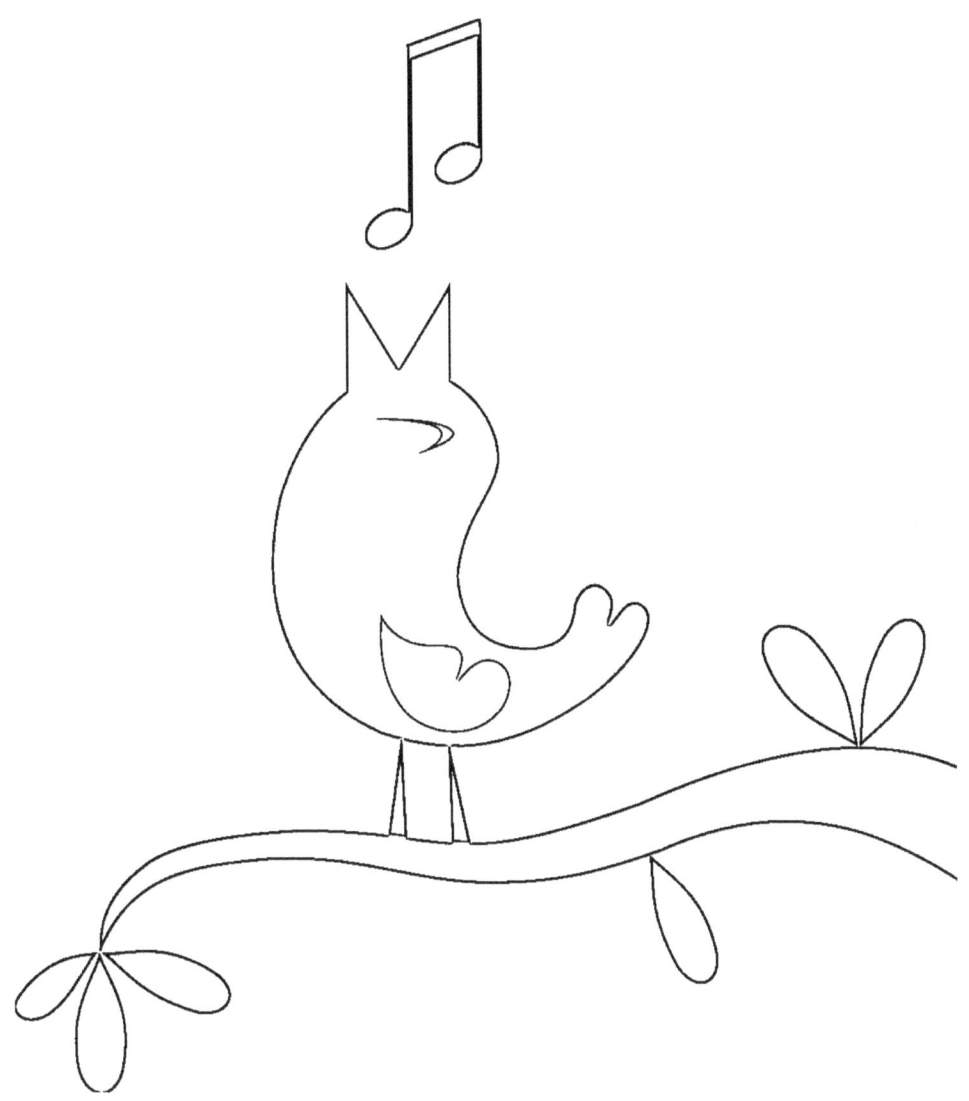

LION

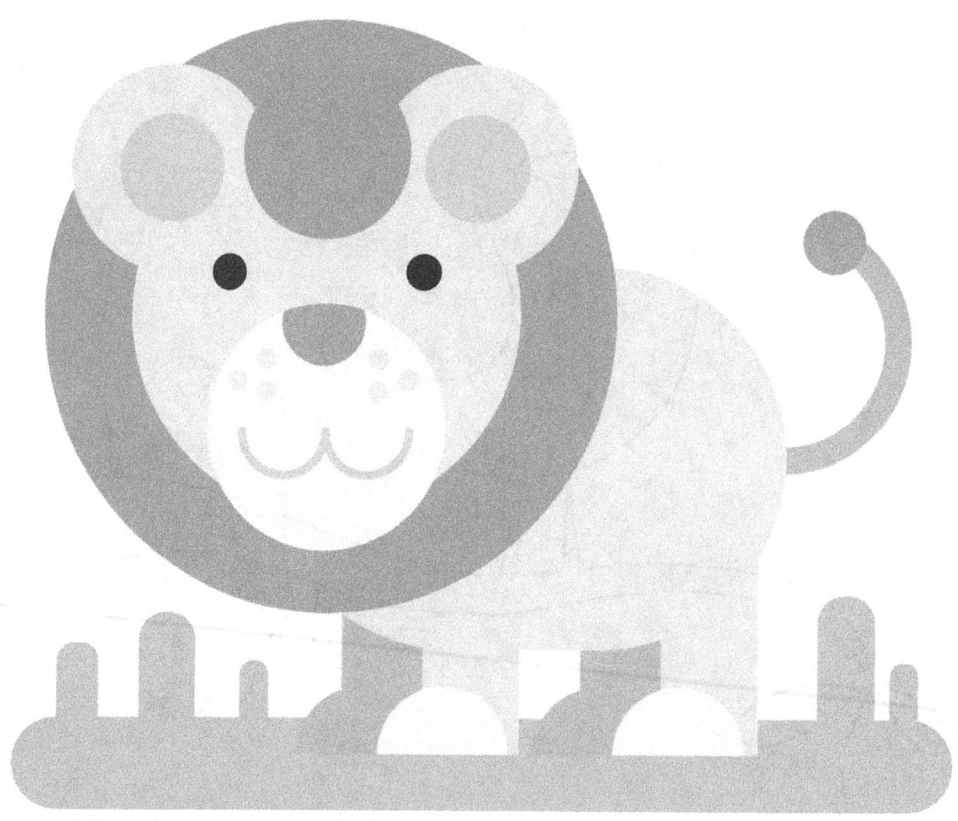

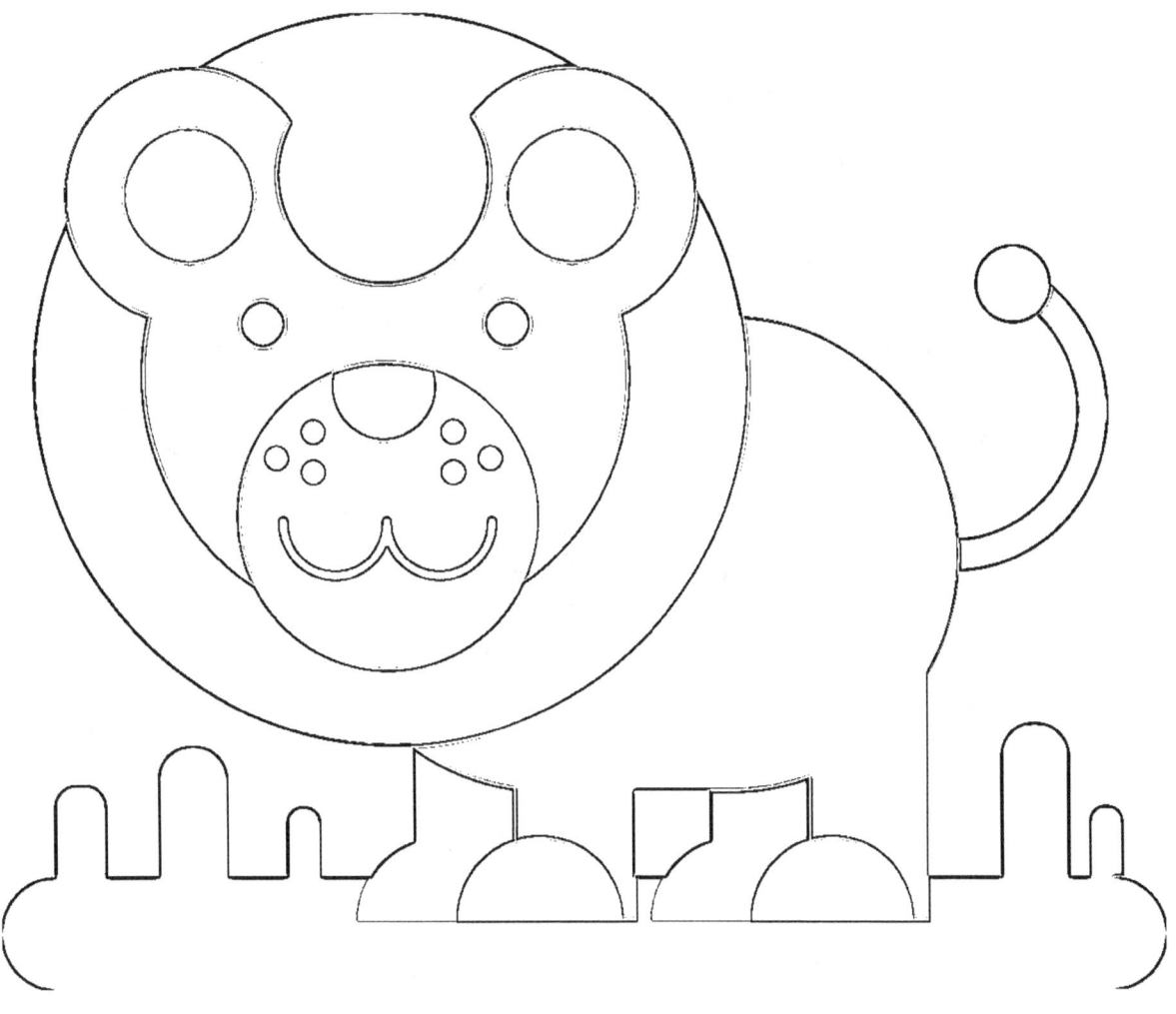

PEACOCK

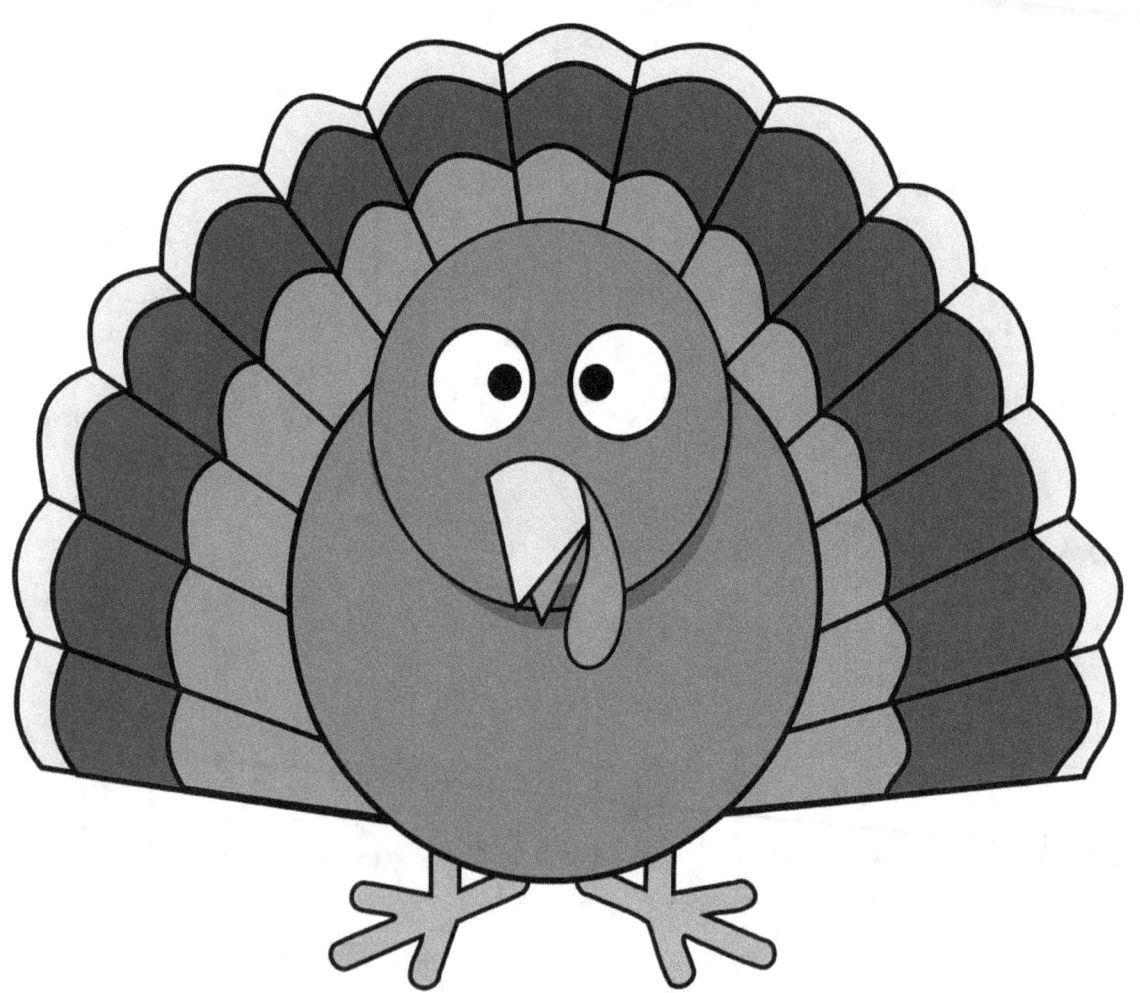

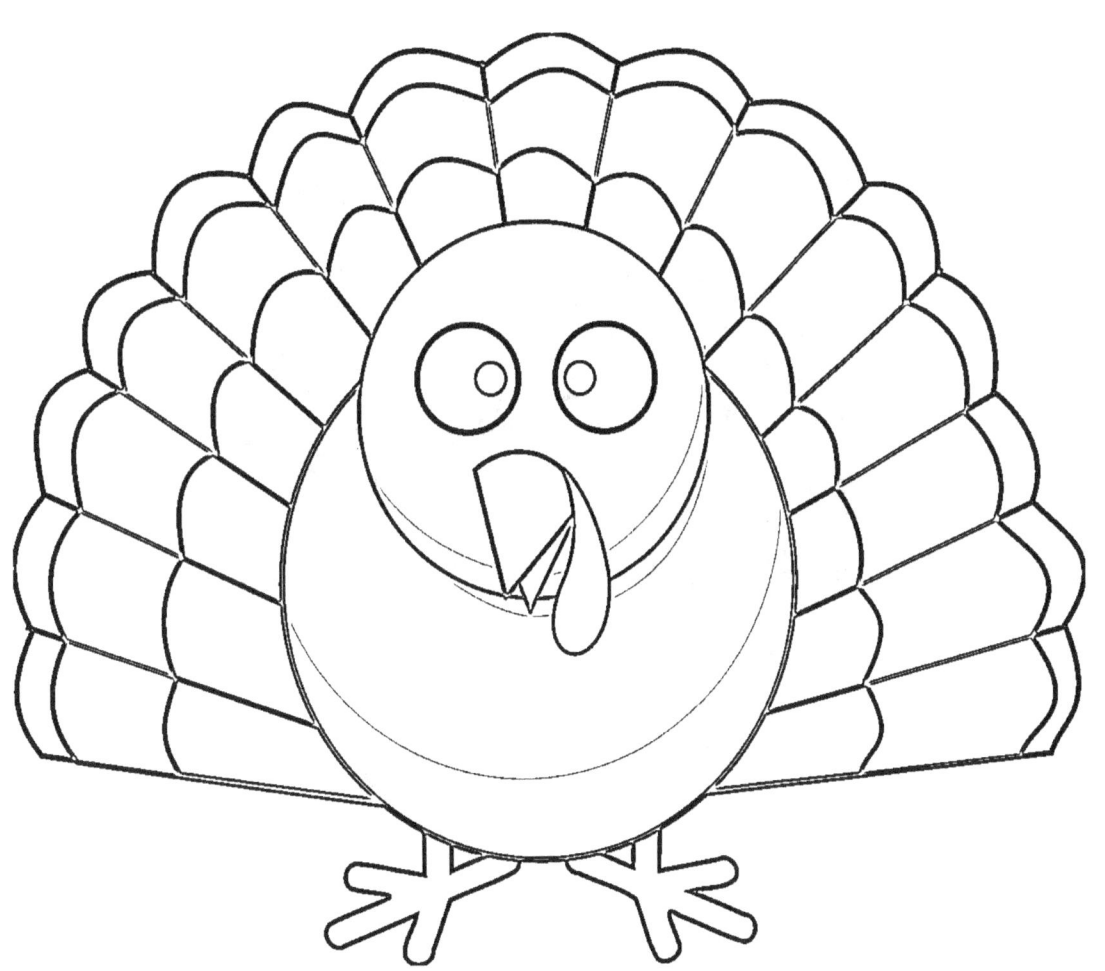

ZEBRA

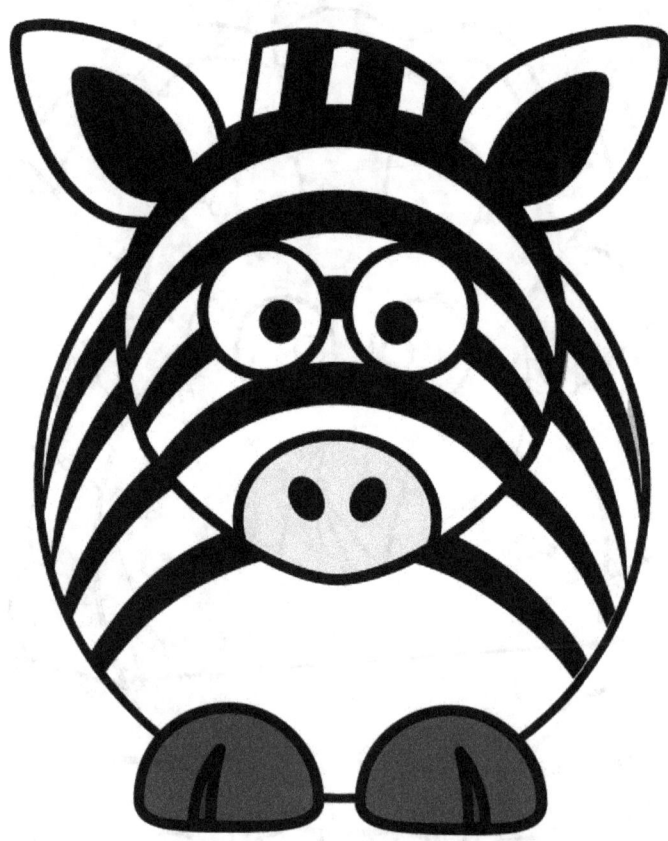

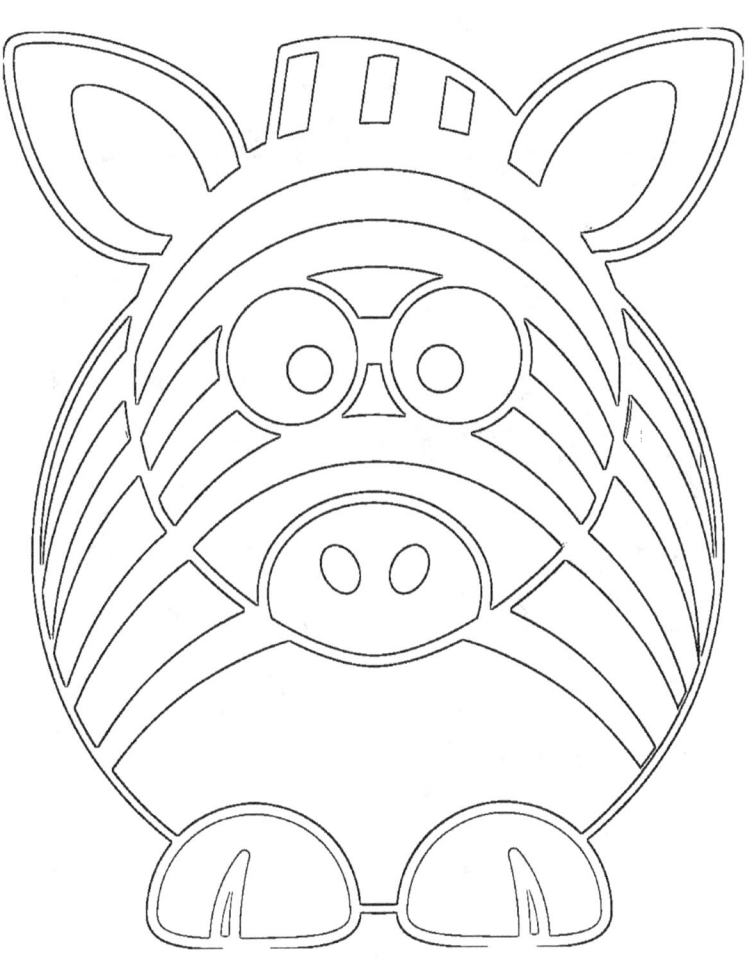

TURTLE

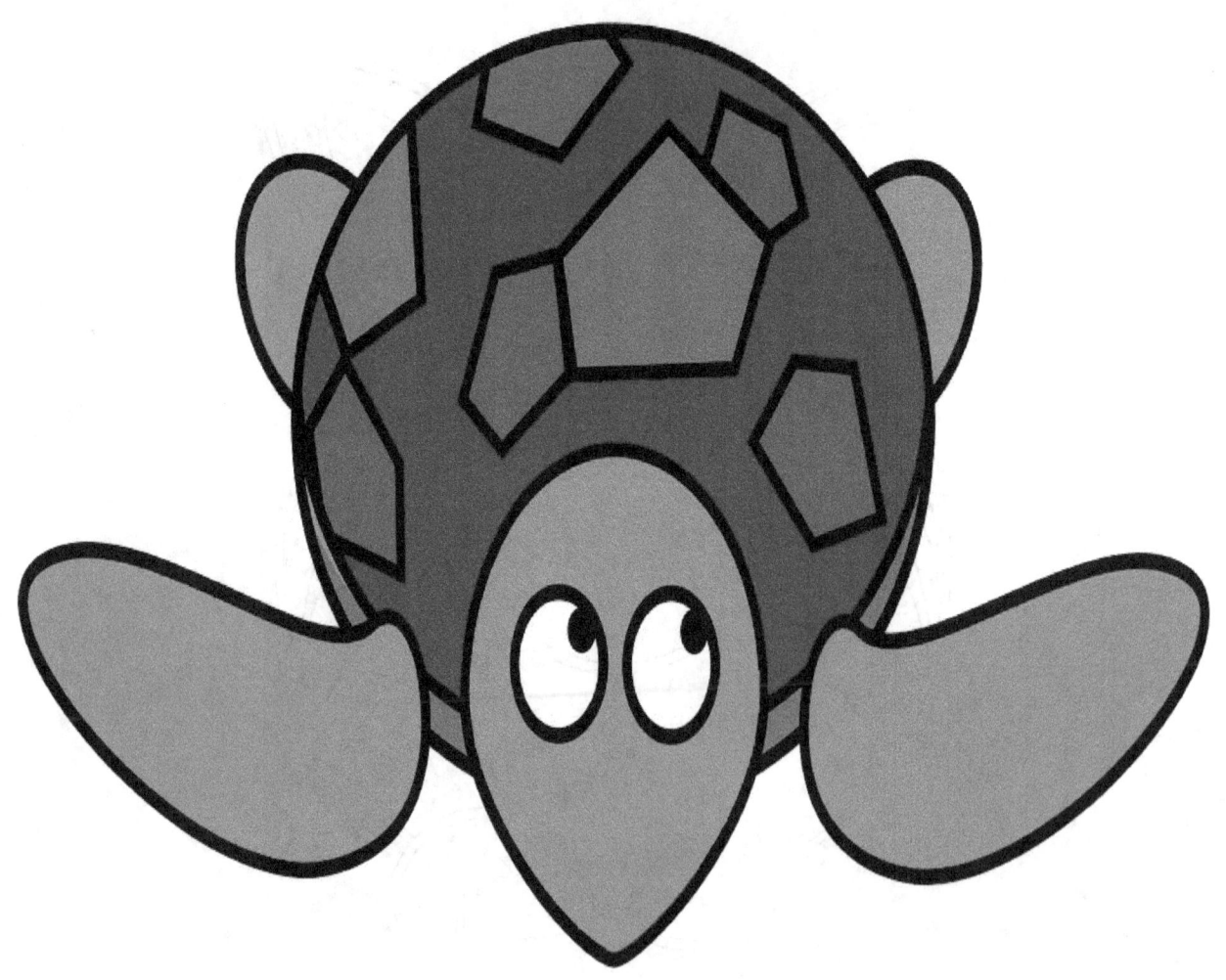

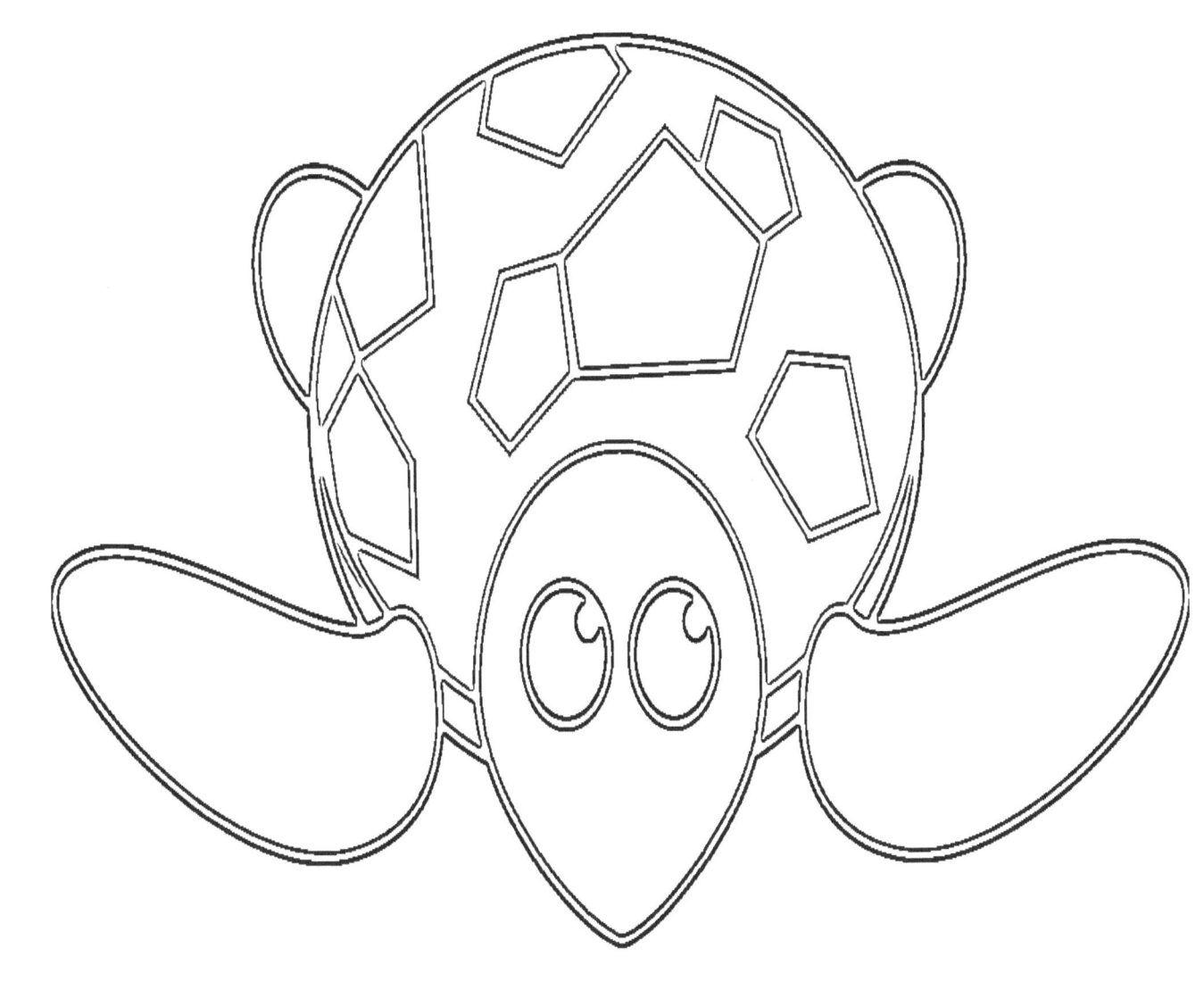

www.ingramcontent.com/pod-product-compliance
Lightning Source LLC
Chambersburg PA
CBHW080528220526
45465CB00006B/2637